Praise for *First and Only*

"Jennifer R. Farmer writes a much-needed love letter to Black women looking to thrive at work and in life. *First and Only* is an essential resource for any career toolkit."
—Minda Harts, author of *The Memo*

"Jennifer R. Farmer is a hell of a coach, and if she is detailing what Black women are experiencing in workplaces, we should listen and then take action."
—Michael Render, songwriter, activist, and rapper professionally known as Killer Mike

"Jennifer R. Farmer could run a boot camp for emerging women leaders. Her coaching exudes urgency, confidence, and care. If anyone can create a trusted road map for Black women in the workplace, it is Jennifer, who has navigated tough terrain with celebrity personalities, politicians, and the 'good ol' boys.'"
—Rev. Dr. Brianna K. Parker, Black Millennial Cafe

"Jennifer R. Farmer is an amazing voice in empowering powerful communications and storytelling to shift the narrative. A brilliant thinker with a knack for eliminating waste, she creates strategies that leverage resources for the maximal impact while cradling the sacredness of one's message. An important and necessary soul for the journey around this nation, proclaiming a new story rooted in equity and inclusion."
—Rev. Ben McBride, co-director, PICO California

"Jennifer R. Farmer is an insightful listener and observer of human interaction. She uses her insights to speak directly to the core issues impacting leadership. Her analysis perceptively integrates gender, race, religion, and overall worldview to offer more nuanced understandings of leadership than the one-size-fits-all approaches more commonly promoted."
—Rev. Dr. Cari Jackson, author; Clergy in Residence, Religious Coalition for Reproductive Choice

"I reached out to Jennifer R. Farmer in a time of crisis. I was a new interim executive director who was overworked and overwhelmed. Jennifer was a lifeline for me during some of my toughest moments. She had excellent practical advice, but she also brought a kindness and compassion for what I was going through. Jennifer brings a wealth of expertise and a high degree of emotional intelligence to her leadership. She's the kind of leader that other leaders like me want to emulate."

 —Rev. Katey Zeh, Interim Executive Director,
  Religious Coalition for Reproductive Choice

"A lot of people do PR, but there aren't a lot of PR people who do it well. Jennifer R. Farmer is the exception. She fuses creativity with a practical and empathetic approach to solving some of the thorniest issues. I love that she is now talking about Black women and leadership. I know that in my work coaching leaders to communicate more effectively, the same rules don't apply to everyone. I've relied on Jennifer as a trusted source for her perspective and guidance and want more people to learn from her. Our workplaces, our world, would benefit from hearing more from Jennifer R. Farmer."

 —Meghan Dotter, founder of Portico PR

FIRST & ONLY

FIRST & ONLY

A Black Woman's Guide to Thriving at Work and in Life

Jennifer R. Farmer

 Broadleaf Books

Minneapolis

FIRST AND ONLY
A Black Woman's Guide to Thriving at Work and in Life

Cover image: Vectorig/istock
Cover design: LoveArts

Print ISBN: 978-1-5064-6684-2
eBook ISBN: 978-1-5064-6685-9

For my daughter, Maya, and my nieces Janay, Ashante,
Renee, Armani, and JeMariah—
May you go without being asked, speak without seeking
permission, and create without fear of failure.

CONTENTS

Part IV Strategies for Healing

Part V Paths to Liberation

FOREWORD

It is time to tell it like it is.

You go into work each day knowing you must prove yourself. From what you wear, to how you style your hair, to how you talk, to what you say, to how you phrase each and every email before pushing send: you are in a constant state of proving you deserve to be there.

This is life for Black women at work. Every single day. Any therapist will tell you this state of being is exhausting and unhealthy. Yet this has been our reality.

Professionally, Black women are habitually underestimated, undervalued, and underappreciated. When we enter workspaces, we enter them knowing that we must prove ourselves. We must convince others that we are good enough, smart enough, capable enough to take on any task or challenge. It is ironic that, given our history birthing and caring for nations, we are still asked to demonstrate our value and worth. Because we often lack respect, we spend our lifetimes proving and reproving ourselves. Unfortunately, this does not get better as we age. It does not get better as we increase our education level or climb any corporate ladder. Regardless of how much we have accomplished, and despite how much we have achieved, we are continually asked to prove that we belong.

This can be psychologically tormenting. And yet many of us do not have the option of giving up or giving in. For one thing, we like to win just as much as the next person. Second, in addition to the responsibility of caring for ourselves, we are often in the sole position of caring for husbands, children, extended family members, and friends. This says nothing of the professional responsibility many of us carry as we build careers, teams, or companies. We come alone, yet we shoulder the burden of many.

It is time to progress, and *First and Only* is that first step.

As Black women, we are often the first and only: the first and only Black woman in the boardroom, the first and only Black woman on the school board, the first and only Black woman as vice-president in a company. First and only can be a lonely, scary, unsafe place to be. Having been a trailblazer on so many paths over her long career, Jennifer R. Farmer has been both "the first" and "the only." Jennifer is asking us to acknowledge where we are positioned in our work lives, with all its limitations and possibilities, and dare to imagine different outcomes. She is inviting us to reclaim our power and our joy by looking at the facts and moving on from there.

First and Only is asking us to progress, even when bowed over with fear. As Audre Lorde said, "When I dare to be powerful, to use my strength in the service of my vision, then it becomes less and less important whether I am afraid." Audre is saying, as Jennifer is saying, that to be powerful is not to live with the absence of fear. It is to move forward despite it. It is to come out on the other side. This book speaks to how we come out whole on the other side. It gives us permission to see our humanity, beauty, intellect, vision, and strength.

For these reasons and more, *First and Only* must be considered essential reading not only for Black women but for people who work with Black women. There are lessons to be learned in every chapter. For me, since the world's stage is my office, the chapter on self-care was an important reminder. It reminded me that while I am strong, I do not have to be a superwoman, too. Through no fault of their own, our Black grandmammas and our Black mommas have been teaching us to be invincible and never crack; this cycle must end. *First and Only* tells us why.

In producing this magnificent work, Jennifer has written a love letter to our foremothers, our mothers, ourselves, and our daughters. She has seen Black women in our beauty, frailty, and humanity. She has honored our history of nurturing worlds and birthing visions. She has spoken to our possibilities of shifting atmospheres and changing environments. Her book is a foundational work, called forth from a deep place of knowing. It will help Black women position ourselves in the universe and walk boldly in our divine appointments.

May you find yourself in the pages of this book. May you see yourself in all your beauty and perfection. May you recognize your greatness. May you discover that which you need to thrive at work and in life. I know I have.

—Nina Turner, speaker, cable news commentator, former state senator from Ohio, and former national campaign cochair for Senator Bernie Sanders' 2020 presidential campaign

PART I

What Black Women Face

CHAPTER 1

I See You

You are the first in your class and, sometimes, the only. Maybe you were the first to go to college, the first to move away from your hometown, the first to have a child, or the first to overcome the odds. You have likely been the only Black woman in more educational settings or professional settings than you can count. You have accomplished more than most people in your family and community have.

As the first, and often the only, Black woman to do what you are doing, you face a challenging road. You are sometimes misunderstood by your friends and family. You enter spaces where few have gone, but those spaces aren't always welcoming. Yet you shoulder on, attempting to do something that few people in your circle have ever done. You are the first, and you have often been the only.

I see you. I see your beauty. I see your work. I see your efforts to hold it all, balance it all, and juggle it all. I see the pain that you sometimes hide and are forced to display. I see your justifiable anger and confusion as it is weaponized against you. I see your anger being mistaken for rage, when sometimes it is sadness flipped inside out. Your contributions may be overlooked and your work undervalued, but I see you. Because you exist, I do too. Because you keep standing, she does too.

This book is for you.

Why I Wrote This Book

This book is not about how to get or keep a job; it's about how to heal yourself so you can sustain yourself. *First and Only* is simultaneously a love letter, a manifesto for progress, and a leadership resource. It is the opening argument to a trial on career advancement, asserting that the path for success for Black women is self-care, self-worth, and a willingness to push for progress even as we fight for our liberation.

I wrote *First and Only: A Black Woman's Guide to Thriving at Work and in Life* for three distinct reasons. First, I wrote this book because I wanted to center the experience of Black women. From our body, to our hair, to our marital status, to our child-rearing, to our professional wages, Black women are inundated with messages that we are not enough. While the world may question the worth of Black women and whether we belong, it is not us: it is them. I wrote this book because I am tired of the gaslighting Black women sometimes experience in the workplace: we are told we are too loud, too bossy, too opinionated, or too Black. I believe the words of Malcolm X when he said, "The most disrespected person in America is the Black woman. The most unprotected person in America is the Black woman."

Despite this, I believe we come from a lineage of women who thrived and overcame the odds. As Ghylian Bell, founder of the Urban Yoga Foundation, once told me: "Black people were dropped off to a foreign land and had nothing, yet they survived and even thrived." That legacy is my legacy and it is yours. In writing this book, I am providing fuel to support you so that thriving is the norm and not the exception for more and more Black women. I'll do this by validating and acknowledging the unique challenges we face and offering solutions to support us.

Which brings us to the second reason I wrote *First and Only*: because the challenges Black women face are unique and varied, we need content that is exclusive and specific to our needs and realities. We still deal with all types of disparities, biases, and issues with upward mobility. Black women still fall behind our counterparts in areas such as pay, maternal health, health disparities, and life span. For instance, Black women had to work until mid-August 2020 to earn what white men had earned by December 2019.

Even our hair is politicized and used as a tool to control and exclude us. The Supreme Court recently declined to accept cases over whether workplace bans on locs are racially discriminatory. Even though the New York City Commission on Human Rights declared its commitment to protect residents' right to wear their hair in dreadlocks and other hairstyles, few cities and states have followed suit. No Black woman is immune to criticism about her hair. In 2017, when Fox News commentator Bill O'Reilly was asked to comment on the speech Congressperson Maxine Waters was making, he said on national TV—and to laughs from most of the panel—that he couldn't hear a word she was saying because he was too focused on her "James Brown wig."

The stress of racism is even adversely impacting our health. The Southern Poverty Law Center found that Black women "have higher death rates for nearly all cancers than white women and are twice as likely to experience infertility problems. These health disparities manifest most severely, however, in maternal death rates—the rates at which women die during pregnancy or up to after a year after childbirth." The organization went on to state that "even when all other factors are equal—economic status, educational background, and access to health care—maternal death rates for Black women are still higher compared to white women." We cannot discount the impact of racism and sexism on the overall mental and physical health of Black women. In too many cases, Black mothers and babies die prematurely because we are not believed and are undermined by health professionals, the very people supposedly trained to give care regardless of the race, socioeconomic status, or age of their patients. When you hear stories of even wealthy and famous Black women having horrible pregnancy and post-pregnancy experiences that could have resulted in them losing their lives, you know that the system as a whole devalues Black bodies. That certainly includes Black women and Black children.

Finally, I wrote *First and Only* because there are so few books that speak to our experiences in the workplace and in social environments. Demographics in the United States are changing. By the year 2050, minorities will become the majority. With an increasingly racially diverse population, leadership styles and approaches will invariably change. What worked for our parents and grandparents, who had different generational customs and worked in less diverse spaces, will not work for us. As our social landscape changes, the policies, modes of thinking, and leadership principles of the past need to change. Authors like me, with various identities, including "Black woman," must come forward. Black women enter the workplace with varied gifts to share and unique hurdles to overcome. We need leadership texts that speak to the duality of our existence—highly educated yet falling behind on key indicators; highly talented yet fighting to be seen and valued.

As leaders think about how to topple mindsets that can be harmful for the workplace, it is important to have diverse thought leaders who are not entrenched in the past. We need leaders with fresh perspectives. The market for leadership and professional growth books has been dominated by white men and, to a lesser degree, white women. It bears noting that many of the leadership development and business gurus are also aging. John C. Maxwell is a phenomenal thought leader, but at some point, there will be a need for the changing of the guard.

Women of color who have leadership development experience, emotional intelligence, and cultural competency are ready, and I fit squarely into this new generation of leaders. I was the first person in my family to attend and graduate from college, and then to earn six figures. I was the first person in my family to write and publish a book. I have entered spaces that my parents could only dream of entering. And in addition to my own experience as a Black woman working in the private and public sector and managing employees for more than fourteen years, I draw on the wisdom of others. I interviewed Black women who are hiring managers, therapists, advocates, and executives to gain insight on how to overcome career hurdles and care for ourselves and our families.

There are a ton of books on preparing for on-the-job success, particularly with a first job. There are fewer that offer insight on what it takes to be successful from a racial justice and racial equity perspective. Leadership books that do not speak to the impact of racism and sexism on upward mobility are like tigers without teeth and claws. Yes, we as Black women need the tips and skills that some of these books provide, but we also must have strategies to address the racism and anti-Blackness that we will surely face. This book will equip you with those strategies. To survive and thrive, we must be clear about what we face and be endlessly devoted to our personal development and self-care.

How to Use This Book

First and Only comprises twenty-seven chapters. The chapters are organized into five sections:

- ▸ What Black Women Face
- ▸ Myths to Resist
- ▸ Truths to Embrace
- ▸ Strategies for Healing
- ▸ Paths to Liberation

The sections demonstrate the work that we must do to thrive as the first and only. You can read this book linearly or select the chapters that most resonate with you. At the end of every chapter, there is a place for you to write reflections, including on how the section impacts you, speaks to your personal experience, or encourages you to consider new ways of thriving. I've inserted this section because I believe it provides for deeper self-reflection and exploration. For some people who struggle with journaling, it may also be an easier on-ramp for documenting one's feelings. Since there are prompts, there is no need to pick up a journal with blank pages, stare at the blank pages, and question where to start. This format may provide a helpful prompt.

Let me take a moment to prepare you for content that may evoke strong emotions. Some of the most difficult things to discuss are faith, politics, and sexuality. I recognize that my discussion of faith in these pages may be problematic for some. There are so many poor representations of religion that the sheer mention of it may be triggering. However, as I share leadership principles and discuss strategies for thriving, I will occasionally reference my Christian faith. I do this to be authentic and because so much of my survival has been about cultivating spiritual practices that work for me. When I am bowled over by the manifestations of racism, it is my faith that reminds me, as Dr. Imani Perry, author and professor of African American studies at Princeton University, writes in her book *Breathe*, "Individuals are the precious bulwark against total desperation—in them we find the persistence of possibility." When I believe all hope is lost, or when I begin to think that safety rests exclusively among my own kind, I remember all the people who are different from me yet who have loved me deeply. Upon reflection, I realize that I cannot abandon the possibility of tomorrow nor shut down the road to redemption.

When I share religious experiences or reference biblical verses, my intention is not to proselytize. And as I advocate for you to be who you are, I seek to follow my own advice. Because so much of how I view the world and interpret my life experience is rooted in faith, I have chosen not to divorce my faith and belief in God from this work. I am who I am, and I will share all of who I am with you.

Everyone has something they wish someone had told them about how to thrive as a Black woman. I want you to share your wisdom with me, with the Black women and girls in your life, and the entire "First and Only" community. You can share your reactions by engaging me on Twitter or Facebook, and, of course, by sharing a copy of this book with the women in your life. The point is: I'd like you to use the book as a launching pad for deeper discussions with the women in your life.

Liberation with a Side of Joy

As you begin to process the experience of being the first and only, my hope is that you experience liberation and joy. While there is a tendency as Black women to take on more than our fair share of responsibility, I want you to remember that it is okay to experience joy and liberation. That means we must sometimes say no to the myriad demands that are presented to us and invest instead in our joy, happiness, and liberation.

Throughout this book, I highlight the perspective of Black women to both document their experience and share their recommendations for how we survive. Building and sustaining healthy relationships with Black women and men is important, and we'll discuss everything from owning your power, building your circle, knowing your worth, and caring for your body with the same zeal that is applied to professional advancement.

On-the-job success comes down to distinguishing what is and what is not yours to carry. It comes down to deciphering the childhood wounds that may impede or slow your success. To be successful in the workplace, you need a deeper understanding of who you are as a person. You need to not only know your internal triggers and childhood wounds but also how to manage them. But as you work on yourself, you'll need to continue pushing the people around you, convincing them that challenging systemic racism is indeed in their best interest. All of this can be incredibly tiring. If Black women are to persevere, we must be endlessly devoted to our physical, mental, and emotional well-being.

Joy is important because all that I describe in these pages can be mentally, physically, and emotionally draining. Without looking for joy, even as an act of resistance, we will be unable to sustain ourselves. One way that I have been able to maintain hope, even when the external evidence suggests I should shut down, is by cultivating a spiritual practice, making a commitment to resist, and tending to my own childhood trauma. I will share that with you in this book. This book is about joy, it's about resistance, and it's about succeeding even in systems that conspire against us. As we navigate life as Black women, we must stare down the challenges while cultivating hope for a brighter tomorrow. As Dr. Perry has said, "The truth is that life is unsafe. And genius, often, remains unvalidated or, even worse, dormant. But joy, even in slivers, shows up everywhere. Take it. And keep taking it."

I hope you'll buckle up and enjoy the ride!

What are you most excited about in reading First and Only*? What is one area you believe you'll wrestle with as you work through this book? How can you ensure you remain open and engaged with this process?*

CHAPTER 2

Why Center Black Women?

A ctress Gabrielle Union is one of the most accomplished celebrities in Hollywood. She has starred in many films and can best be described as Black America's sweetheart. Talented in her own right, she is also married to NBA player Dwayne Wade. Yet none of her accomplishments or accolades protected her from racism's reach. She was terminated from NBC's *America's Got Talent* after raising concerns about a toxic workplace.

As a judge on the show, Union raised concerns about Jay Leno allegedly making a racist joke about Koreans and requested that the show's executive producer, Simon Cowell, not smoke in his dressing room. Very quickly, Union was labeled a "problem." A November 2019 article in *Variety* reported that Union received a half dozen notes over the one season she was on the show saying her hairstyles were "too Black" for the *America's Got Talent* audience. Another ousted judge, Julianne Hough, who is white, also allegedly received near-constant criticism about her hair, makeup, and wardrobe.

Women in general are judged not only based on their professional ability but also on their physical appearance, including body shape, weight, wardrobe, makeup, hair texture, and hairstyles. Black women must deal with the double whammy of being a woman and a person of color. So, whereas we may be judged on several factors outside of the skill set assessed via a job description, we also experience the impact of racism. Some of us have been battered by colorism, the mechanism by which the hue of our Black skin provides yet another entry point to exclude, dehumanize, or exoticize us.

While all women can experience sexism, Black women must navigate several terrains just to earn a paycheck and support themselves and their families. In 1989, when Dr. Kimberlé Crenshaw coined the term *intersectionality* to describe how different identities overlap, she recognized that there are multiple layers of marginalization; this concept clearly explains what African American women face. She must have done so to note the need for equity, meaning offering of specific renumeration based on the unique circumstances various individuals face.

I am centering the experience of Black women with racism and sexism because it is too easy for society to blame problems at work on Black women like they did with Union. When people malign Black women as being angry or problematic or "too Black," they do so because such narratives benefit them and permit them to access power.

Further, many Black women experience additional intersecting oppressions, such as marginalization for being LGBTQ, differently abled, or otherwise labeled. For Black women who are LGBTQ, or Black people who are gender nonbinary, there are additional challenges based on multiple fronts including gender, sexual orientation, and race. They not only deal with the joy and pain of standing in their truth, they are often put into a position where they are asked to fit in, forced to fit in, forced to explain, or forced to teach others. Imagine the inner work a nonbinary person must do just to survive and thrive in a world that refuses to see them or is set up not to see them. Everything around them is prearranged to challenge their own vision for their lives. A member of the LGBTQ community in a cisgender, heteronormative environment will face all the hurdles I describe above and some that I, as a cisgender heterosexual woman, cannot begin to imagine. Media reform and social justice activist Malkia Devich-Cyril explained it this way:

> As a Black, queer person who is butch, I then experience another layer of oppression: on the one hand patriarchy, denies me and undermines me, and on the other hand, I am told I am a beneficiary of patriarchy. Do you feel me? Because I am a stud, I then am the purveyor of patriarchy. It's a very complex place to be, particularly in my field [where] there is no other people like me. My field is primarily white even though my organization is primarily of color. Trying to navigate all those different terrains and barriers has been a complex and draining journey.

Who Is This Book For?

The leadership book you are holding is written for Black women who have scanned, without success, their bookstores for content that addresses gender and race. It is for people who have done all that the standard leadership book advises, yet still receive negative feedback that is racialized and gendered. This book is for the Black women who have been told, over and over again, "a rising tide lifts all boats." It is for women who experience crude comments based on their hair, body type, and communication style, yet have little guidance for how to process, respond, and move on from such harmful situations. Finally, I'm writing to Black women who have had the experience of being first and only and who have not been able to go to loved ones and friends because, while sympathetic, they are unable to relate.

I am seeking to comfort Black women who have struggled to find their experiences represented in business or how-to books. What we need to thrive at work is different from what our counterparts need. Black women need texts that speak to the reality of our bodies, our hair, and our speech being policed in a world that has been trained to deny our humanity. While many may read it and draw insights from it, I want Black women to know that I wrote this with them in mind.

It also is written for the leader and the organization that want to create safe spaces for Black women to do good work and be their authentic selves. Since there are few courses that offer a cultural and contextual framing for Black women to succeed in the workforce, I wrote this book with the hope that it will fill the gap.

I am centering Black women in this book by narrowly focusing on Black women, as opposed to lumping Black women into a broader discussion of women of color. Women of color indeed face unique challenges, and those challenges are different based on race. For instance, the closer a group is to white, the more socially acceptable they are. It doesn't mean they don't experience oppression, but their journey is different from Black women in a world that is anti-Black by default. It has always annoyed me when companies tout diversity because they have Asian Americans on staff—and not a single Black person. I must question such environments, especially when the company management believes they are "fine on diversity."

Anti-Blackness

I also want to be clear that much of the treatment Black women experience has to do with sexism and anti-Blackness. While this may not be a popular thing to say, it is true that other women of color can be deeply anti-Black. This can be reflected in expressions of disdain for Black women, cultural appropriation, and contributions to harmful stereotypes. To talk more broadly about women of color without clarifying my intention of centering Black women would be to dismiss the anti-Blackness that exists among many Latinx, Asian, and other people of color toward Black women.

What am I talking about? In an October 20, 2019, opinion piece for NBC Think, writer Christina Tucker, who cohosts the "Unfriendly Black Hotties" podcast, elaborates on anti-Black racism across various races and ethnicities: "While it can be tempting to want people of color to work together against white supremacy and racism, anti-Black racism is persistent in all communities, not just white ones. . . . There is a danger in assuming all minorities are the same, in assuming the struggles of someone who is Latinx are like the struggles of a Black person."

Tucker's essay was in reference to actress Gina Rodriguez, who has a history of eyebrow-raising comments regarding Black women in particular, and Black people in general. For instance, after the blockbuster movie *Black Panther* came out, Vox Media reported that Rodriguez said in July 2017, in a now-deleted post: "'Marvel and DC are killing it in inclusion and women but where are the Latinos?! Asking for a friend.'" While it is appropriate to advocate for inclusion of underrepresented and marginalized groups, to do so on the backs of another marginalized group is inappropriate.

Further, after Miss South Africa Zozibini Tunzi was crowned Miss Universe in December 2019, many non-Black Puerto Ricans highlighted their own brand of anti-Black racism. In a column published by NBC Think, writer Susanne Ramírez de Arellano noted that "José Pastrana, a supervisor for Special Education for the island's [Puerto Rico] Department of Education, posted a racist message on his Facebook page calling Tunzi 'La prima de Shaka Zulu,' ('the cousin of Shaka Zulu,' a South African military leader, though; she is no relation)." And María Celeste Arrarás, host of Telemundo's *Al Rojo Vivo Show*, said the pageant was meant to measure beauty, not IQ, which was interpreted as saying that Miss South Africa was not beautiful. Again, proximity to whiteness is valued in many non-Black people of color.

Further, the Black Youth Project challenged Ariana Grande in February 2019 for cultural appropriation throughout her career: "To many, Ariana does not appear to appropriate Black sound and aesthetics because she has utilized an incremental strategy as opposed to introductory or overnight turnaround into Blackness. Grande's stardom and musical sound have stockpiled on elements of rap and R&B from the very start of her commercial musical career."

Author Ijeoma Oluo, who wrote the best-selling book, *So You Want to Talk about Race*, described why cultural appropriation is so damaging:

> The problem of cultural appropriation is primarily linked to the power imbalance between the culture doing the appropriating and the culture being appropriated. That power imbalance allows the culture being appropriated to be distorted and redefined by the dominant culture and siphons any material or financial benefit of that piece of culture away to the dominant culture, while marginalized cultures are still persecuted for living in that culture.

For these reasons and more, I did not write a book for women of color. I am centering Black women by focusing on and speaking directly to our experience, because that experience is undervalued and rarely celebrated, even among people we might think would be our allies.

Style

In addition to centering Black women, I made an intentional decision to capitalize the *B* in the term *Black women*. Prior to the broader racial reckoning following the murders of Breonna Taylor, George Floyd, and Ahmaud Arbery, this practice was inconsistent with many style guides. However, most style guides weren't written with Black women—or Black people, for that matter—in mind. At this point in my life, I echo the words of Dr. P. Gabrielle Foreman, who wrote on Twitter, "Capitalizing the proper name of my own Diasporic people feels so fundamental that I didn't clear it up front for several pieces + projects I'm about to finish."

Capitalizing the *B* in Black is about *seeing* an entire demographic: a people who have long been ignored, especially by the systems that govern how we show up in the world. In addition to many style guides recommending against capitalizing Black, some also discourage the use of titles. For instance, the Associated Press Stylebook advises against putting the "Dr." title before a person's name if they are not a physician. However, one of the tactics racists used to degrade Black men and women was stripping away their titles and refer them as "boys" or as "girls." This was designed to chip away at their agency, autonomy, and accomplishments. Obtaining PhDs and advanced degrees is difficult. When a person has overcome hurdles to do so, I want to honor their sacrifice and celebrate their achievement as much as possible. One small way to do this is to put the "Dr." before their name if they have obtained a PhD, and to include their political title if they are an elected official. These are intentional acts of awareness and resistance.

Why Does Any of This Matter?

Racism may look different today than it did in the 1940s, 1950s, and 1960s. But it exists, and it is pervasive. If we are to thrive, we must reframe how we think about ourselves and our accomplishments. We must move beyond the belief that technical mastery alone guarantees success. Without a comprehensive view of ourselves, our role in the world, and how racism and sexism affect the places we live and work, we will not build the stamina nor the reservoirs of support necessary to position us for long-term success. Without an abiding commitment to spiritual practice, it will be difficult to overcome the challenges that we face.

Additionally, few of us grew up in perfect families. Even if we believed our families of origin did everything right, the people around us may disagree. Depending on your family's background, you may enter the workforce at a profound disadvantage. For instance, if you grew up in a family that used silence as punishment, without unlearning, you may use silence as a weapon in the workplace. If you grew up in a family that struggled to communicate what was working and what wasn't, and if you haven't invested in therapy and coaching to help you unlearn this pattern, you may have difficulty communicating your needs in the workplace. If you grew up in a judgmental family, where you as well as others were constantly judged, the frame through which you view other people will be judgment. Without intervention, that will play out as judging yourself, judging others, and withholding compassion for yourself and others.

Without intentional work and deprogramming, we will bring the same unhelpful patterns we grew up with into the workplace. We will not have what it takes to thrive over the long term nor be able to coach and support other Black women in doing the same. We may take positions that expose us to trauma versus positions that will feed our spirit. This book prepares you to do just that.

Perhaps you have it all figured out. Perhaps you are already doing what I suggest in this book. If that is the case, share this book with others. Share it with the woman who you believe is struggling. Share it as a conversation starter. Share it as a gift for a mentee. If you are already filled, use this book to fill others.

What practice have you adopted to help you navigate being the first and only?

CHAPTER 3

Hostile Work Environments and the Choices Before Us

My sister has made a career in commercial property management. She was once employed by one of the largest commercial real estate companies in the U.S. Her office space was nestled inside a beautiful building, which testified to belonging to a well-resourced company. Yet she experienced a level of racism that while we know it exists, put her on her heels. Mentally, she wondered how she would cope. Physically, she began to experience headaches, stomach discomfort, and severe anxiety on Sundays before returning to work. After nine months of verbal insults by and threats from management, she quit. When she did, she didn't have another job waiting for her. She preferred to face unemployment than endure a toxic workplace where she felt unwanted and unwelcomed. She made a painful choice, but she did so for her mental and physical well-being.

Many Black women enter the world of work with something to prove and someone to *dis*prove. If we were raised to believe that we were less than, we want to prove everyone wrong. For those of us who have been taught that we need to work twice as hard to be considered half as good, we may work ourselves into the ground attempting to fulfill this mandate. For those of us who want to live up to the legacy and the hopes of our families, we are focused, dedicated, and inspired to work as hard as possible. When we do what we think is right and what our families of origin have suggested, and consequently experience success at work and in school, we are surprised to realize that racking up degrees, promotions, opportunities and experience doesn't always translate to acceptance or the ability to truly exhale. We still enter spaces where people expect us to fail and get upset when we don't. We may have fatter bank accounts or more resources than we did when we began our careers, but that doesn't mean that we are treated with the respect or given the authority commensurate with our experience or position.

I will never forget taking my daughter to her first dental appointment. The hygienist was white and the dentist was Black. The hygienist cleaned my daughter's teeth first, and then the dentist came in to examine my daughter. Yet the hygienist failed to acknowledge her seniority or experience level. The hygienist did all the talking. She finished the dentist's sentences, talked over her, and took up so much space that I was literally shocked into silence. I kept looking at their uniforms, the age difference (the hygienist was definitely younger than the doctor, which I assume means she was less experienced). Her privilege was on clear display.

I kept wondering if she was aware of, or concerned with, how she was appearing. Moreover, I wondered if the dentist pulled her aside after the appointment to tell her that her behavior was inappropriate.

Those of us who grew up in poverty are determined to ensure our families don't experience lack the way we did. Those of us who have experienced overt racism in the workplace may have moved beyond the trauma, yet we may still experience aftereffects such as self-doubt, anger, and depression. In many cases, we carry the weight of wanting and needing to succeed in workplaces, even though many of those spaces weren't set up for our success. To be clear, workplaces that are not actively working to be antiracist and antisexist are not set up for our success. Leadership books that are silent on issues of race, sex, and gender cannot speak to the unique needs of Black women.

As we enter professional workspaces, we enter with a cultural legacy and understanding that may be different from our coworkers'. While many of us have enjoyable experiences, practically everyone reading this book has experienced, or will experience, racism and sexism in the workplace. In this book, we will look at ways that racism and sexism show up in noticeable and subtle ways. We also will examine strategies for navigating hostile work environments, up to and including removing oneself from such environments.

Let's be clear: A hostile workplace doesn't have to be one with overt violence. When you hear the word *hostile*, you may think of the most egregious forms of oppression. But a hostile environment is one with explicit and implicit bias. It is one where there is overt discrimination, yes, but more subtle types of discrimination—being overlooked, undervalued, and uninvited—create hostile work environments as well. People who call themselves liberal and progressive may still be anti-Black, racist, sexist, and hostile to Black input and expressions. In a phone interview, entrepreneur and political commentator Tezlyn Figaro describes it this way:

> In my career as an entrepreneur, often as the only Black woman in the room, I have noticed that Black women are rarely seen. Although white women may feel ignored in the workplace, my experience has been that not only were they seen but they were also heard. Whereas Black women aren't seen, heard, or valued. Although we stand out in the room literally, our experience, our perspective, our diversity of thought are ignored and unvalued, and often we are not even recognized as living beings at the table. When I do speak, often people pretend to listen but disregard everything I say.

One of the most fundamental human needs is to belong and to be accepted. Regardless of how much we have accomplished, we still want to be accepted, and we want to belong. So, it is important to consider the full range of harmful environments.

Strategies

Many Black women have experienced the pain of being overlooked or having our observations discarded, and we have experienced it in multiple jobs. So, it is important not to minimize the trauma that blatant disregard for Black women, or women who are different than the norm, can have.

We have a choice in how we respond. As Black women, when we move and operate in hostile work or social spaces, we develop conscious and unconscious coping strategies that are influenced by our backgrounds, professional experience, and even unresolved wounds. Some strategies serve us better than others, and some work in some situations but not all. For instance, I have been in hostile environments, and my response in some situations was to turn inward, to shut down. I learned, however, that eventually all the pent-up frustration and agony was going to boil over. I would say something and say it in a way that was destructive. Sure, I may have backed people off me in the immediate moment, but the longer-term consequences of the blow up were disastrous. In other situations, I would confront the challenge head-on without mincing words. In these scenarios, I was often told that I needed to "be nicer."

We may choose different strategies at different times. Depending on our background, personality, and experience, our responses to racism and sexism lead us into one of several camps.

Assert Ourselves Boldly

Some of us boldly stand for what we believe in and proudly assert ourselves in as many situations as possible. Sometimes when we do this, we are reluctantly listened to and let in. Other times we are ignored or our colleagues placate us, telling us what we want to hear without any intention of honoring or acting on our requests. Our colleagues may belittle us or deem us too outspoken. But when we have brought our full selves to the table, we experience satisfaction. While we may not be able to change the outcome of various situations, when we advocate for ourselves, we show up for ourselves. We stand with and for ourselves and this, my friends, is power. As Audre Lorde said, "I have come to believe repeatedly that what is most important to me must be spoken, made verbal and shared, even at the risk of having it bruised or misunderstood. That the speaking profits me, beyond any other effect."

Bend and Contort

Some of us bend and contort ourselves into microcosms of who we used to be, erasing our identity and the very aspects of our personality that make us unique. Fearful of being called an "angry Black woman," the label often used to silence and shut Black women down, we may withhold our truth, tolerate abuse, or fail to persistently advocate for what we need to succeed. To avoid this label, we may tolerate microaggressions, sexism, and other forms of subtle abuse. This can lead to social anxiety. Psychologist and professor Angela Neal-Barnett reports that coping with the "angry Black woman" and the "strong Black woman" tropes can lead to social anxiety. "In workplaces, college, and professional school settings around the country, Black women often find themselves the only one or the first one," she writes. "In these situations, they have been taught that they have to be twice as good to go half as far, that they are representing the race and that they are being watched more closely than their white counter-parts; beliefs that are not necessarily inaccurate. These beliefs coupled with the Strong Black Woman image increase risk for social anxiety."

When we withhold our truth, a part of us dies. We remain quiet and "go along to get along"—a tactic I have employed and many of you probably have too. While this approach may work for a time, it is not the path to freedom and happiness. It is a form of denying oneself, and such denial can lead to depression and resentment. We must be careful about thinking our silence will protect us. It will not.

Disengage

Others turn inward and vow to do the bare minimum in order to keep the paychecks coming. Sure, we show up to work, but we will not offer ideas, tell the truth about how we're feeling, support our colleagues, or work to advance the organization's mission. In some cases, we show up and are less productive because our minds are focused on so many other things. If we are not mindful, we will show up and do everything except what we have been hired to do. In these situations, we watch the clock, waiting for the end of the workday. We go to meetings but remain silent, or we give surface-level responses to deep, probing questions. We turn the pain of our work experiences inward. While this may work momentarily, it can also lead to depression, melancholy, or destructive coping habits. While some of us may seek relief through therapy, some of us turn to addictions to food, improper relationships, shopping, or other sources.

But as the title of Dr. Bessel van der Kolk's book so succinctly states: *The Body Keeps the Score*. We become depressed, we engage in self-destructive behaviors, or we withdraw completely. We may still be physically present in the workplace, but we shut down. Our bodies are there, but our creative genius is long gone.

Overwork

Those of us who were raised with an overinflated sense of responsibility may work to fulfill all that is on our plate— even when doing so compromises our health, happiness, and well-being. When we choose this strategy, we attempt to be all things to too many people. In the process, we burn out or lose our spark.

Some of us internalize the negative feedback and begin to see ourselves the way our critics see us: without context, compassion, or concern. When this happens, we practice negative self-talk. Our internal chatter is so destructive that we wouldn't feel comfortable uttering these same words out loud or to a friend. We spend time ruminating about whether our supervisors and colleagues are correct about us. We wonder if we have been wrong about ourselves and tell ourselves that perhaps we're not that talented after all. For instance, during one era of my working life, I experienced a pregnancy without the support of my child's father; had another child who was arrested in a very traumatic experience; and was simultaneously navigating a new job. I was getting feedback at work that I needed to be "nicer" and that my approach was too harsh. I was given this feedback at the exact time that I was under-resourced. Given where I was in my personal life, I lacked the capacity to meaningfully act on the feedback I was receiving and instead shut down. I was being judged without context and expected to perform as though these traumatic circumstances weren't occurring.

The point that I want you to keep in mind is that if you are in a hostile work environment, your body, psyche, and spirit will respond. If you are not conscious about how you will protect yourself and cope with the environment, or leave the environment altogether, you will default to old patterns of coping. If you do not seek support from a counselor, therapist, friend, or trusted colleague, you will feel isolated and unsupported. As you reach out to others to help you make sense of these experiences, the mere act of speaking to people who are not a part of your organization will help you sort out the work that belongs to others and the opportunities, even in the pain, for you to grow.

At one point I was working for a wonderful organization whose mission I believed in, but I was severely short-staffed. One of the ways I coped with the pressure of work was engaging in body care during nonwork hours. This included Senegalese West African dance with a wonderful dance troupe, Thiossane, in Columbus, Ohio. I also joined a local fitness center and participated in kickboxing, yoga, and spinning. It helped that one of my colleagues joined me for the kickboxing class. These activities enabled me to keep work in proper perspective rather than allowing it to consume my consciousness. They also provided a way to release some of the stress associated with work that was stored in my body. This was a conscious way of coping with a tough work situation. It was also an approach that didn't cause further harm to me or the people around me. The caveat here is at the time, my oldest child was living with his father, so I had more spare time than the average single parent. The good news is some of these activities can be done at home before children awake or after they have gone to bed. Should your financial situation permit you to hire a babysitter, doing so could also give you pockets of time to exercise and engage in body work.

Why This All Matters So Much

At the height of the #MeToo movement, during which mostly middle-class and upper-income white women shared harrowing tales of sexual abuse, the accounting firm Ernst & Young (EY) organized a leadership training for its female executives. The one-and-a-half-day course was offered after a partner at the company went public with sexual harassment claims. It was supposedly an "empowerment" workshop, but it ended up being something else entirely.

Numerous sources, including HuffPost and the *Chicago Tribune*, reported on what was said. "Women's brains absorb information like pancakes soak up syrup so it's hard for them to focus," the attendees were told. "Men's brains are more like waffles. They're better able to focus because the information collects in each little waffle square." Women were also allegedly told, "Don't flaunt your body—sexuality scrambles the mind (for men and women)."

It is hard to believe that in the twenty-first century, a reputable firm such as EY would sanction such problematic and sexist content. But this underscores my point that leadership texts and talks must speak directly to the needs of women without centering men in the process. They must be mindful of race and given by people consciously doing their own antiracism work. They also shouldn't be delivered or offered by people who hate the subgroup in question. I'd argue that the facilitator of the EY talk—regardless of whether the person is male or female—disliked women and distrusted them at a fundamental level. Why else would they say women had smaller brains?

As we saw in chapter 1, many leadership books were written by white men without the needs of women in mind, let alone the needs of Black women, who navigate the landmines of race, sexual orientation, and gender. This book was written by a Black woman for Black women. I will acknowledge that I am writing as a heterosexual Black woman whose social location includes single parent, system impacted, and squarely middle class. Yet my perspective as a woman and as a Black woman illuminates what I believe many leadership texts and leadership workshops get wrong. When Black women are not told to complete one more thing, we are given outdated advice to fix ourselves rather than to expect more from the environments we work in, or from the men and non-Black women around us. For instance, we have been told not to be argumentative, not to show emotion, not to discuss our families or their needs—essentially to become robots without cares, concerns, or priorities. If leadership books are not emphasizing the layers of our existence and speaking to the trauma that we have faced collectively, and if trainings are hostile, then they perpetuate harm.

What about a Person's Manager?

Shouldn't a person's manager be teaching her this stuff? Isn't a supervisor supposed to be coaching workers in all the leadership, professional growth, and workplace success strategies that we'll cover in this book? Sure, and in an ideal world they would.

But this question presupposes managers have done their own antiracism work and are not only proficient at the technical aspects of their own jobs but evolved on issues of racial justice too. Researchers Alyssa Croft of the University of Arizona and Toni Schmader of the University of British Columbia at Vancouver found that "stigmatized students sometimes fail to receive the critical feedback necessary to identify areas needing improvement, particularly when evaluators are concerned about appearing prejudiced." These researchers gathered their data in academia, but the same findings bear out in the corporate world. Black women are not receiving the coaching and support they need to grow and advance. Moreover, managers must have the mental space and work capacity to lead. Yes, managers should be coaches, but when managers' plates are filled to the brim and overflowing with their own portfolio, they may not have the bandwidth to simultaneously coach and mentor their teams, let alone tend to the needs of diverse team members.

Additionally, managers are flawed like everyone else. A promotion to a leadership role reveals less about a person's growth and evolution as a leader and more about the individual's capacity to perform well in one or more areas. If you find one or two enlightened managers throughout your career, consider yourself lucky. We simply cannot assume we can or will get everything we need to be an effective employee, leader, or contributor from the person to whom we report.

Regardless of what coping strategy any of us choose in any given moment, and regardless of how much coaching or support we receive from our supervisor, many of us carry our own trauma. Black people are 20 percent more likely to experience mental health challenges than others but less likely to receive treatment, according to the Office of Minority Health. Further, racism is a form of trauma, as are sexual abuse, car accidents, and living in areas with high incidences of crime and physical and domestic abuse. When you factor it all together, most Black people are entering the workplace traumatized. Some of us desperately want to do a good job and to deal with the hostility, visible and invisible, that gets thrown our way at work. But sometimes, we can carry emotional baggage from childhood, past employment situations, and life that weighs us down.

What You Can Expect

If you are tired just reading this, you are starting to get the picture. The question remains: What is the best way to respond? What can we do? As we think about what it means to be the first and only, we must also be cognizant of the myths that have been shared to supposedly help us "make it." The next chapter analyzes some of the myths that have been passed along to Black women, and the reasons those myths are problematic.

I want to note that part of what being "first and only" means is that you are on a path that the people closest to you have not traveled. While they may want to be helpful, they may lack the context to do so. This is not to say that you can only take advice from people who have excelled or moved to places where you have not. I believe there is wisdom in all of us; everyone has something to teach and learn. I am essentially saying that in the quest to help, some people have given advice that might work for other environments but not as much given where we are as a society or where we are in our career. The next chapters explore the myths we may need to reconsider.

What is a myth that you believe you should analyze more closely?

PART II

Myths to Resist

CHAPTER 4

You're Good at It,
So You Should Do It

You are fabulous, and you are multidimensional. Your talents may not be limited to one or two areas. Yet just because you are good at something and people recognize your gifts in that area doesn't mean you should invest all your time there. Too many times, we wait for external validation and praise to decide that we are good at something. When we receive praise, we may drop what brings us joy and focus on the thing that others recognize. But what if the talent they recognize is only a part of your skill set and not your greatest gift? What if what others recognize is not what brings you joy?

When I was trying to wrap my head around this idea of being told you are good at something and therefore feeling pressure to do it, I called up my friend and former colleague,

Dr. Baranda Fermin. Baranda is the type of person you want in your corner. She is bright, well read, empathetic, and courageous. Naturally, when I want to understand some of the things that hold Black women back, I reach out to her.

I was trying to reconcile having skill in one area but also feeling burned-out. Dr. Fermin said something that I'll never forget: "One of the things I wish I would have learned earlier is that what you are good at, what comes easiest, may not be what keeps you joyful or motivated as a leader," she said. "I am often invited into spaces based on gifts people see me do with ease. After the initial process, I have found myself in a rut. I'd think, 'I'm good at this,' 'I'm in demand,' 'my ego is being stoked,' but that isn't enough."

How many of us have had this experience? Further, many women leaders have this idea that we should wait to be invited. Baranda says she was "getting invited into spaces where I was not being fed creatively. Being invited in didn't feel the way I thought it should. I needed more room for creativity. I learned that even the things we don't call creative—technical writing, Excel docs—still have a creative nest, and I need that creative nest."

This sounds similar to something I heard gospel singer Leandria Johnson confess in a March 16, 2019, episode of OWN's *Iyanla: Fix My Life*. Johnson has an angelic voice. She can bring people to tears, applause, euphoria, and surprise in a matter of seconds. She first won my heart when she competed on BET's *Sunday Best* hosted by Kirk Franklin, so I was surprised when I heard her confess that she didn't want to sing gospel music, which is how most people know her. Perhaps she epitomizes what my friend Dr. Fermin was talking about.

"I realized that being good at something doesn't always lead to fulfillment," Dr. Fermin said. "It did not mean I was going to be motivated enough to push through barriers that would inevitably come. What I'm good at isn't necessarily the thing that makes me the most creative or happy person. I required balance and diversification of my own portfolio, and I think others do too."

Do Your Own Discovery

To further illustrate Dr. Fermin's point, I looked at my own career. I am a communications strategist who writes, edits, pitches reporters, and advises and trains clients to successfully participate in media interviews. When people see my clients getting media attention, they want to hire me to help them get media attention. But media pitching is only a part of my job; it is not the center of my work. I have been in situations where I have taken on so many clients who solely wanted media pitching services that I found myself drained, discouraged, and disappointed. Media pitching is tiresome work. If it consumes more than 30 percent of my business, I am in trouble. Over time, I have learned to be judicious and careful about which clients I take on for media pitching work and how long I'll work with them. I have found that shorter-term pitching contracts work better than longer ones.

In case you need reminding: you are talented, and you are multidimensional. Don't let others determine where you should plant and grow and how you should use your time. Do your own self-discovery, and then decide how you want to focus your energy and how much of yourself you want to give to your various gifts.

Have you ever sat down and wrote about what brings you joy? Take a moment and jot down what brings you joy professionally.

CHAPTER 5

Anger Is Harmful

When I was growing up, anger was scary. I feared expressions of anger. I wanted everything to go right so my mom wouldn't get angry. I learned to anticipate what she and others might want to please them. For her part, my mother was poor, had a host of health problems, and was responsible for raising three children. After our parents divorced, my mother was left in the home with us. While our father was present, I know life was hard for her. I also know that I never wanted my mom to be angry. As I grew up, I learned to see anger as a bad thing. Rather than expressing anger directly, I turned it inward, or I would hold onto to anger and express it at the point when it morphed into rage. This led to a host of relationship challenges and conflict-avoidance challenges. As an adult, I am re-examining my relationship with anger, how to express it constructively, how to withstand the anger of the people I love and respect, and how to determine if my anger is really a screen shielding other emotions.

With this as a backdrop, I'm wondering: What have you been taught about anger? How did your family of origin express anger? Was anger frowned upon, celebrated, or rarely shown in your family? Was there space for Black anger? More specifically, was there space for Black women to be angry? How do you express anger now, and are you comfortable doing so?

The answers to these questions will shed light on how you manage and negotiate your own experiences with anger and expressions of anger. Where Black women and anger are concerned, there are five things you must know:

1. The people around us are best able to give feedback on how they experience our anger.
2. In a white supremacist world, Black anger is almost always seen as dangerous and dreadful.
3. Anger can be healthy. It is an indication that a boundary has been crossed or that a need is not being met.
4. At times, anger may be the outward expression, but the internal experience is depression.
5. The "Angry Black Woman" trope is rooted in bias and white supremacy.

The People around Us Can Share Feedback on Our Relationship with Anger

There are things I've learned about myself that I've only learned from the people in my life. My children, team members, friends, and family have been the mirrors I needed to see that when I express anger without thought and intention, it is harmful. In the same way that I dreaded my mother's expressions of anger, the people I love have dreaded my expressions of anger. There was something about my upbringing and my inability to express disappointment constructively that was bringing harm on the people I cared about. I suspect that this may be a lifelong challenge, but it is one that I am aware of and actively working to address. When you are looking for feedback, especially examine how the people with the least power in your life relate to you. If they communicate fear, dread, or anxiety about coming to you, that is an indication that there is a problem in the relationship.

Black Anger Is Viewed as Dangerous

We live in a world rife with white supremacy, and in such a world, Black anger is almost always seen as dangerous and dreadful. There is a reason that Brandt Jean, whose brother Botham Jean was fatally shot by Dallas police officer Amber Guyger, received an award in December 2019 from law enforcement after he hugged Guyger following her murder conviction. Guyger was off duty when she entered Bothem Jean's apartment and shot and killed him after allegedly mistaking his apartment for her own. Following Brandt Jean's decision to hug Guyger, the internet was set ablaze with news stories on forgiveness and the meaning of this young man's hug. White supremacy is comfortable with forgiveness but threatened by anger.

Because Black anger is viewed as dangerous, many people are uncomfortable when others become angry even when anger is the only suitable expression. They attempt to stifle it, and they label people who are angry as problematic.

Moreover, when Black women express anger or disappointment in the work setting, they are viewed as scary. For instance, when I was a supervisor giving feedback to white women, they would sometimes cry. I know other Black women who have had similar experiences. Knowing my personal background, I always examine whether my upbringing is showing or whether there are racial dynamics at play. When I have gone to great lengths to be less threatening and still receive input that I am, indeed, scary, I wonder which factor is at work—race or personal background.

If the feedback I receive from some of my own supervisors is "to be nicer and less scary," I question what niceness means in a society primed to see Black people as scary. "Niceness is another form of violence. It is a white construct," according to organizer, consultant, and writer AnaYelsi Velasco-Sanchez at a 2019 Liberating Evangelism conference. For Black women and women of color, the guidance to "be nice" is used to deny our humanity, silence us, and have us "go along to get along." I am also not sure how to be nice when our very presence invokes fear and when our mere opinions elicit outrage.

When you are labeled angry, think about the worldview of the person making the accusation. Then think about your personal history and the feedback you've received about your impact on others. Finally, ask if there is validity to the feedback or if it is rooted in racism or sexism.

Anger Can Be Healthy

There are many misconceptions about anger. Many people are uncomfortable when others express anger. They wonder whether they are safe. They become defensive. They judge the person who is experiencing the anger. But anger can be a warning light. It is an indication that a boundary has been crossed. It can also be a reaction to one's needs not being met. Before we harshly judge anger, we should remember that it can be healthy and necessary. It is so necessary that everyone experiences anger. When people are uncomfortable expressing their anger, they turn it inward. In fact, depression is said to be anger turned inward. It is necessary to give voice to our feelings—even the feelings that aren't pleasant. Unexpressed feelings are stored in the body, and the person who suffers is the person unable to name their displeasure. The other people who suffer are those on the receiving end of individuals who have inadequate methods of communicating when they are upset.

Anger Is Sometimes a Manifestation of Depression

While Black women are often called angry, anger is an appropriate response given the circumstances in many cases. I recall watching an episode of *Iyanla: Fix My Life* titled "House of Healing: The Myth of the Angry Black Woman." In this episode, Ms. Vanzant invited Black women to share space in a house, ostensibly to shed the "angry Black woman" label. As I watched the various cast members, I realized that, to a person, all had experienced deep trauma. One cast member said that her grandmother told her that "her father was too black and that she would come out with nappy hair and be ugly." She went on to recount an experience of being threatened by drug dealers and not having a father to call to for help.

When I heard this story, and that of other women on this show, it offered so much context to their outward behavior. If the saying "the body keeps the score" is true, why would we expect people to continually bear trauma without signs of scars? Famed novelist Zora Neale Hurston once said, "If you are silent about your pain, they will kill you and say you enjoyed it." If those words are true, it makes no sense that Black women are labeled angry for vocalizing pain. These women aren't just angry; they are hurting.

How true is this for you? It took me years to realize that depression was manifesting itself as anger. In 2017, I was forty years old and carrying a baby without the support of the child's father. I was beginning a new job where my talents were underutilized. I also had another child who was in crisis. In every sense, I was flailing. I am quite sure that I was unpleasant at work. I am also sure that my colleagues at the faith-based organization where I worked at the time demonized me. But I was so depressed I could barely function. As a Black woman, however, I still needed to perform, earn a living, and do so while being pleasant. On many occasions, I felt I couldn't rise to the task.

The "Angry Black Woman" Trope Is Rooted in Bias

Many times, when Black women are called angry, the label is less about us and more about how our presence makes other people feel. Sometimes when Black women are called angry, such labels are rooted in bias. Black women in this situation should assess whether we are indeed angry or depressed; then we must ask if we are experiencing the impact of bias and white supremacy.

Finally, when it comes to the "angry Black woman" label, it is a subversive trick to silence Black women and get them to go along to get along. Fearful of having this dreadful label cast upon us, we will keep silent when we really should be screaming, or we will retreat when the situation requires that we fight.

A Solution

What has helped me navigate this complex terrain of anger, depression, and bias is vulnerability. When I have allowed myself to be vulnerable and share with others some of what I am going through, I have gotten closer to receiving what I needed. Further, at points when I was not willing to be vulnerable, even in safe spaces, I had to unpack why. I realized that part of the legacy handed down to Black women by the people in our lives is to be strong, to take whatever is handed to us, and to suck it up and push through.

Malkia Devich-Cyril is a queer Black woman who has been a pioneering force for media reform. I have been in sessions with her and literally could listen to her all day. She is learned in every sense of the word. She is a deep thinker, and it is impossible to be in her presence and not leave having expanded your knowledge and understanding. I spoke with her about the code that is passed down from Black woman to Black woman, and this is what she shared:

Black women have been doing a lot under extreme conditions for a very long time. And my mom is just one example of that. You know? How Black women have been taught to think about their labor is really something else. Black women are taught that we labor at any expense, and every expense. You just keep going. You just do it. Whatever the "it" is—whether it's husbands, whatever. That has always been the mantra, and the thing that you hear repeatedly. At least I did. You just have to keep going. You don't succumb: you don't succumb to pain, you don't succumb to grief, you don't succumb to illness. You don't do anything that would make you have to stop. That lesson has made me very ill in my life. It's also made it possible for me to do things I never thought I could do.

This means that showcasing vulnerability or telling someone what we need on an emotional level can feel like weakness. But it is precisely what we need to be healthy and whole. When I make a choice to be vulnerable, I can shed the façade of the Black woman as superwoman. There is something very freeing in being able to say, "Hey, I'm having a really hard time right now," or "My reaction right now is less about you and more about my present circumstances."

Additionally, when we are willing to be vulnerable, we free others to do the same. When I have walked in my truth, other people have shared with me how my decisions allowed them to make decisions in their own best interest.

As you move through life and work, if you are called an "angry Black woman" or tempted to call someone else "an angry Black woman," consider whether anger is a shield for depression and sadness, remnants of their childhood, or a reflection of your own unresolved work.

What has been your relationship with depression and anger?

CHAPTER 6

We Can Be Everything to Everyone

From childhood, many Black people, women included, were taught that we needed to work twice as hard to be considered half as good. But this advice is setting us up for an *L*: a loss. Black women have embraced that mindset at our own peril. We have tried to outwork, outsmart, and out-think everyone around us. Black women continue to obtain higher education degrees at rates higher than women of other races and Black men according to the National Center for Education Statistics. Even though as a group we are highly educated, we remain stagnant when it comes to wages and compensation. Studies show that Black women continue to earn sixty-two cents for every dollar a white man earns.

In our quest to make it, defy the odds, and stand out, we sometimes take on too much, fail to set healthy boundaries, and say yes when we really should say no. If we are not careful, we will shoulder the weight of the world, but that is God's job, not ours. As a single Black woman with some degree of financial and positional privilege, I can easily fall into the trap of attempting to be everything to everybody. It is easy to overestimate my abilities. But at some point, I must ask myself *why*. Why can't I say no? Why am I saying yes? How do I benefit from agreeing to do too much? What is my motivation? What is my ego getting in return, and can I live in an environment where I am not consistently noticed or celebrated?

If you want to be healthy and grow professionally, you must unpack your reasoning for wanting to stand out. If you are trying to live down word curses, which are negative things people have spoken about or to you, or if you are trying to prove the people in your life wrong, take a step back and ask yourself whether standing out is worth it. That is why television actress Grace Byers's book *I Am Enough* is so influential. It teaches young girls—and quite frankly, women—to accept themselves just as they are, without modification. At its core, it offers the lesson that we are enough. We do not have to perform, and we do not have to perpetually check off one box after another after another.

Striving to stand out can lead to unhealthy competition and an erosion of the team dynamic. I have seen this in my own life and career. On conference calls with other communications consultants or with companies that have hired me, I have sometimes rattled off a list of accomplishments and victories to appear smart or talented. When doing so, I haven't always sufficiently given credit to the people who helped propel me and my work to victory. It was all about me. At the end of such monologues, I have asked myself, "Why did you do that?" and "Now what did that accomplish?" I have pondered who I was really trying to convince of my worth: them or me?

Rather than doing the work that is truly ours to do— such as ensuring that we are prepared for opportunities from an educational and experiential standpoint—we can get so caught up in distinguishing ourselves from others that standing out becomes our singular focus rather than mission or service or values. When this happens, we can lose sight of the very things that bring us joy and alienate others in the process. We can get so caught up in the game of being seen that we stop checking in with ourselves and saying, "Sis, is this what you really want?"

Ask Yourself Why

If you find yourself in the pattern of trying to stand out and needing to be seen, ask yourself why. Ask yourself if you really believe in your gifts and calling. If you believe in yourself, perhaps you wouldn't work as hard at gaining external validation. Don't get me wrong: I understand, that as Black women, we are often undervalued and underestimated. But at some point, we must, as my friend Dedeon Jackson of San Antonio, Texas, says, "return that which is not ours to carry back to others with dignity and assignment." For people who will never believe in our worth, we do not have to continually assert it or educate them on why we matter. Now, on the other hand, if you're trying to convince yourself, you will never be able to accomplish enough to develop self-worth. Self-worth is less about what you do and more about how you feel about who you are. If your efforts to stand out are about trying to convince others of your worth, ask yourself why you are giving someone else that much power.

In a world filled with racism, sexism, misogyny, and anti-Blackness, if we measure our self-worth by external standards, we will never stack up. Further, what someone else thinks of you is really their concern, not yours. Our path to excelling at work and in life lies in self-acceptance and radical self-love.

If you can identify with what I've said and believe your efforts to stand out stem from diminished self-worth, I have an excellent resource for you: Dabrena Gandy's *Sacred Pampering Principles: An African American Woman's Guide to Self-Love and Inner Renewal*. In addition to sharing practical, cost-neutral activities for caring for the body, the book offers beautiful affirmations that support self-love and self-acceptance. Because if we do not heal this wound, we will struggle with finding contentment in our accomplishments and give power for our well-being and state of mind to other people.

How often do you attempt to stand out? Have you considered your motivation for doing so? In moments when you've been able to let go of the motivation to stand out, how did it feel?

CHAPTER 7

We Must Ask Permission

Do not ask for permission for something that you have the latitude and the authority to do. Get really clear on your responsibilities, your manager's expectations, and the rules for the organization in which you work. Once you understand these things, you can perform your job without constantly seeking approval. This means that you do not ask for permission to bring a new idea to the table. You do not ask for permission to spend money on an item if the expense is within the pre-established limits for which prior approval isn't required. You do not ask for permission to lead.

When you begin the cycle of asking permission for things that are within your authority to do, you are headed down a slippery slope. For starters, you condition your managers that you will constantly seek their approval. This could go one of two ways. For managers who want you to be more autonomous, constant approval-seeking will get irritating and they may question whether you are able to fulfill your role. Alternatively, you could unwittingly condition your manager to expect you to seek approval for everything, which could lead to delays or the gradual erosion of your authority.

There have been many times in my career where I have given away my power by seeking approval to do something that was well within my purview to do. This is a poor use of both your and your manager's time. If you overstep your boundaries, your manager or another power broker in the organization will notify you. Moreover, you do not have to worry about overstepping your boundaries if you are clear on your manager's expectations from the start.

If you are not sure how to approach *not* asking for permission, set up a meeting with your boss and ask what types of things the manager wants to approve and what types of things you should handle. Then periodically arrange discussions to determine if the way you are leading and exercising authority is working for both parties. You will either receive affirmation or indication that changes are required.

Why Do We Ask for Permission, and How Do We Overcome This Habit?

I wanted to figure out why some people struggle with needing permission, so I reached out to a therapist in northern Virginia. "Many people who need permission for things that are in their purview struggle with self-concept," licensed marriage and family therapist Brittani Strozier told me. "When people struggle with self-concept, or negative thought patterns, they have difficulty with self-validation. They may experience troubling automatic thoughts and cognitive distortions."

Negative thought patterns are very common, she says. "Individuals who find themselves unable to give self-validation should be more aware of their cognitive biases."

Did you grow up in an environment in which you were able to exercise autonomy, or was the environment tightly controlled? What thoughts and patterns do you now have that prevent you from giving yourself permission?

In my experience, I have struggled with chasing perfection and struggled with wanting to please. Both dynamics can lead to "all-or-nothing" thinking and a preoccupation with whether others approve of me and my decisions. But I am learning that rarely can things be purely one way or another. All-or-nothing thinking is damaging. Not only does it limit our options, it also doesn't allow us to celebrate the accomplishments we do make. For instance, if a person's performance falls short of perfection but they have gained valuable insights in the process, there is cause for celebration. Yet all-or-nothing thinking can influence them to see themselves as total failures.

Poor self-concept is another "common culprit" of excessive permission-seeking behavior, Strozier added, and this poor self-concept can lead to overgeneralization. "Overgeneralization occurs when a person picks out one negative event and uses that situation as the standard," she told me. When a person overgeneralizes, they view everything and everyone from the lens of one person or one event, and this negates the possibility that something positive will emerge.

All of this underscores the importance of examining and paying attention to permission-seeking behavior. If you have read this and realize that you struggle with seeking approval for things that are within your purview, think about why that is. Is your need to receive permission tied with something from your childhood or upbringing? If you have lived in a strict environment where your parents or caregivers displayed an autocratic leadership style and where you were not allowed to do much without prior consent, this experience likely shapes how you show up in the workplace. If you lack confidence, you may also need others' validation to make decisions and feel good about those decisions. On the flip side of the equation, if you work with someone who is threatened by the leadership of others, the culture may frown upon people exercising their agency and power. You need to know this to determine whether the company is a good long-term fit.

Are you someone who perpetually asks for permission? Why do you think that is?

PART III

Truths to Embrace

CHAPTER 8

We Are Always Choosing

I was speaking with writer and activist Hannah L. Drake about the moment she knew it was time to walk away from a work environment that was harmful. Hannah worked as an administrative assistant to a pastor. The pastor was to have a meeting one evening, and Hannah went to the janitorial staffer to ask him to set up the room for it. In what turned into a heated exchange, the janitor took an envelope and hit Hannah in the face. When she told the pastor what happened, he threatened to suspend her.

Hannah had been the victim of a workplace assault. She did what women are often encouraged to do: she reported the assault. Yet she was being penalized. In that moment, Hannah knew that it was time to walk away. She knew she was done.

When it comes to choice, there are three things you must know. First, regardless of what the circumstances around you suggest, you always have options. You always have a choice. Next, regardless of how much you accomplish in life or how far you climb up the corporate ladder, you will never get to the place where you do not have the capacity to make a bad choice. It doesn't matter who you are or how much good you have done in the world; you always have the potential to make a choice that will result in horrible consequences. Finally, as Black women, we must know that our choices will always be subject to scrutiny. We do not have the luxury of adopting a "let the chips fall where they may" attitude. The consequences we face due to a bad choice may be more severe than consequences others face.

On the first point: when it comes to thriving at work, Black women must remember that we are always choosing. Even refusing to make a choice is, in fact, making a choice to remain stuck or to maintain the status quo. If you are at a crossroads in your personal or professional life or are mired in a crisis, you may be rolling your eyes at this statement. I will admit that in the past I have gotten so angry when counselors, spiritual teachers, or friends would push me to analyze my options and consider the choices in front of me. If I was gripped by fear, I felt rushed to make a decision, telling myself, "I have to do this," or "I don't have time to consider all the options; I have to take the first one that's being presented." In other situations, I would be going through a terrible situation thinking, "The lesser of two evils is still evil, so do I really have a choice?" But like an onion, there are multiple layers and possibilities beneath the exterior surface.

For instance, for years the narrative I carried about my life as a noncustodial mom was that I didn't have a choice and couldn't afford to fight to regain custody of my child.

This was not true. It was a story I embraced to make myself feel better. One choice in the situation would have been to work multiple jobs to afford a better attorney. Another choice, which is the choice I made, was to give up custody for the sake of my and my son's peace and to help me maintain financial solvency. The story I told about losing custody wasn't entirely true. While it is true that I lost temporary custody at the outset of the trial, I regained custody at the conclusion of the trial and made the decision that, for my mental health and for the health of my wallet, I would return custody to my son's father. While my son did live with his father for most of his childhood, and while it was heartbreaking and stressful, I made the best choice I could given the information, spiritual maturity, and knowledge I had at the time.

One of the reasons I'm emphasizing that we always have choice is because this frame of thinking shifts us from operating from a position of victimhood to one of power. When I believed I didn't have a choice, I told people I lost custody of my son. That was not accurate. It also made me feel bad, like I failed or had done something wrong. And trust me: allowing such thoughts and feelings to grow unchecked leads to poor self-regard, dis-ease, bitterness, and pain. More importantly, given the way I set up the story in my mind, I felt victimized, depressed, and powerless. Changing our perspective to better appreciate our capacity is not only empowering, it also helps us feel better about the choices we do make.

And while we do have choice, we must remember that with choice comes responsibility. Each choice must be carefully made with an understanding that it is indeed possible to do the wrong thing, or to do the right thing at the wrong time. This understanding is important because each of us can, and often has, made poor choices. Further, yesterday's successes and good decisions aren't inoculation from mistakes and wrong choices in the future.

Mistakes Are Easier Than You May Think

Each time I read about a scandal involving a respected leader or celebrity, I ask myself why. Why would the person do what they were accused of doing? And if such an esteemed person made such a mistake, how can the rest of us protect ourselves?

The reminder that we can make grave errors, even after periods of success, is reinforced by the story of former Baltimore mayor Catherine Pugh, whose downfall was ironically related to what started as a good deed. She wrote a series of children's books called *Healthy Holly* to promote healthy lifestyles to young readers. When Pugh was elected in 2016, I am sure she came into office with hopes and aspirations of changing her city for the better. Many elected officials do. Three years later, she was accused of using her position as an elected official to steer sales of her self-published books. Mayor Pugh reportedly earned over $800,000 over eight years for her "Healthy Holly" series from companies that she held power over. The University of Maryland Medical System reportedly gave her $500,000 for 100,000 books; Kaiser Permanente spent $100,000 for the mayor's books at the same time it was seeking to close a real estate deal; and Associated Black Charities paid nearly $87,180 for 10,000 books, even though it only received 4,500 books.

Pugh eventually resigned, citing medical reasons, yet she left office disgraced and and facing criminal charges. By November 2019, she was indicted and later pled guilty to conspiracy to commit wire fraud, tax evasion, and conspiracy to defraud the United States. In February 2020, she was sentenced to three years in prison.

The companies and organizations that purchased her books were also subject to questioning. Having worked closely with Associated Black Charities, which was the inaugural fiscal sponsor of the Baltimore Children and Youth Fund, I know the strain Pugh's investigation had on the team. To assure the public that there was no political influence in the management of the fund, Mayor Pugh's successor, Bernard Jack Young, ordered an audit of the Baltimore Children and Youth Fund and Associated Black Charities, who was the inaugural fiscal manager overseeing the fund. While the audit found no instances of impropriety, the process itself cast a shadow over the work, spurred questions, and slowed the distribution of grant fund dollars to grantees.

The situation with Mayor Pugh left me on my heels. It is tempting to think that mistakes are reserved solely for the young and inexperienced. They are not. Mistakes are an equal opportunity employer. It is a fallacy to think that as we learn, we always improve. Learning requires vigilance and humility. Understandably, the more power, or access to power, one has, the greater the propensity to make errors and lapses in judgment and believe that one can get away with them.

Moreover, we are in a constant battle of right versus wrong. You will never get to the place where you do not have to choose between right and wrong. Making a series of good decisions does not shield you from making potentially disastrous decisions. A history of being ethical is not a defense against future ethical lapses.

Mayor Pugh is in her seventies, in jail and facing law enforcement control upon her release. I say this with no sense of celebration: I mourn for her. Her hopes of having a positive impact on the city have been derailed. For the rest of us, this is a cautionary tale: that regardless of how high we rise, we must still be vigilant in making good choices every day. And given racism and gender bias, Black people and Black women will continue to face disparities in profiling, sentencing, and parole. This will impact our punishment.

As we navigate life and work, we do so with a commitment to understand and explore all our choices. We do so with the realization that giving up our choice is a form of giving up our power. Finally, we navigate life and work understanding that our choices can create opportunities or take them away. We live and work while appreciating that choice is all around us.

Is there an area of your life where you initially thought you had few choices, but now you've reconsidered?

CHAPTER 9

Fear Keeps Us Stuck

Do you know what it's like to be governed by fear? Or to live with fear as though it is a constant companion? Certainly, all of us experience fear occasionally; but when fear becomes all-consuming, it becomes dangerous and debilitating. Perhaps you can imagine what I mean: to be fearful of living authentically, fearful of living a lie, fearful of whether you'll be accepted, fearful that danger will befall you or someone you love. Regardless of the season, fear is a heavy garment. It weighs us down and leaves us feeling like we're suffocating. It steals peace of mind, and it promotes a downward spiral into panic.

When I find myself stuck in a cycle of fear, I try to remember that fear was never God's design for me. Even in situations that rightly provoke pause, God does not intend for me to be so afraid that I'm unable to move. Part of what I grapple with, and I encourage you to grapple with if you struggle with fear, is how to experience fear and yet keep moving. How can we acknowledge that a situation is causing fear and then think about what action to take in the moment to ensure continued progress?

One of the reasons fear is so damaging is that it keeps us stuck. It can also cause us to rush to options that may seem good in the moment but amount to nothing more than a temporary fix. This could include accepting a position that pays well below what you need to survive, agreeing to a project that you have no interest in completing, or indulging toxic relationships out of fear of being alone. Fear breeds desperation. In hindsight, I can say that most decisions I have made in desperation have turned out terribly.

This leads me to conclude that professionally, a major enemy in the workplace is fear. You cannot perform well at work if you live in a state of fear. If you are fearful of making mistakes, fearful of offering ideas, or fearful of your supervisor, you cannot contribute fully to the company for which you work.

Telling the Truth

Years ago, I worked for a labor union in Ohio. The experience was like none I had ever had before and none I have had since. The employees were vocal and fought passionately when there were political or strategy differences. On my first day, I watched the political director, a woman, and the president, a man, in a heated exchange. The president was furious about something, and the political director traded jabs with him without skipping a beat. I was amazed by her ability to make her case, even in the face of a hostile audience. I marveled at her ability to speak truth to power—literally. I was astounded by her willingness to take a chance and not only challenge the organization's leader but also do so in the presence of others.

Now, I am not recommending you pick a profanity-laced fight with your boss. But I do think being fearless in the workplace affords a certain level of power and credibility. To me, being fearless is not the absence of apprehension. Rather, it is a willingness to champion what is right despite fear. It is the ability to move ahead even when doing so creates fear. At that stage in my life, if that labor leader had been angry with me, I would have been befuddled by his anger and disoriented by the fact that he shared his fury while others were present. The employee he was arguing with was able to maintain composure and fight fire with fire, on that and other occasions. I once asked her if she was ever afraid and how she managed to handle herself in those situations. She told me plainly: "You have to be willing to be irreverent." That was her secret. She was unafraid, and she was willing, as she put it, to be irreverent. I have never forgotten that advice.

Most importantly, when we can shed fear, we can tell the truth. Throughout my career, I have worked with many powerful and influential leaders—from politicians to celebrities to movement leaders to world-renowned clergy members. They have had audiences with people of authority. In fact, they have *been* the authority. When I think about these such leaders, one pitfall they must constantly avoid is failing to make sufficient and consistent space for people close to them to be honest. Too many leaders have "yes" people around them—people who say what they think their boss wants to hear. This can be dangerous because it shields leaders from the truth about what is happening around them. I have often tried to be the leader who will speak the truth to clients, colleagues, and supervisors. As a communications strategist, I literally watch some clients' social media pages, and I tell them if their messages run counter to their overall objectives and whether I believe they should take them down. It takes a lot of courage to call up a celebrity or movement leader I'm working with and say, "I don't think that post reflects who you are; I think you should delete it." But I've done it.

Again, I am going to carefully pick my battles and determine on a case-by-case basis what is worth my energy. But being able to place fear aside enables me to speak the truth, and hopefully to speak it in love.

Leadership Can Be Lonely

One of my close friends, Leslie Pierce, owns several tax companies and franchise restaurants. He also works full time and has a staff who manages his business enterprises. He is a devout Christian and doesn't mind who knows it. Everything in his life is measured through the lens of how it stacks up with the Bible, his personal instruction manual. I've asked him how he navigates fear and the overall secret to success. He responded that fear is the enemy, explaining, "In the workplace, once you are fearful, you are inhibited and likely unable to offer your true opinion. If you are overly fearful, you will not treat your boss or other influencers like people."

His words made so much sense. Leadership is often lonely. You are privy to information you cannot share. You receive the brunt of criticism when things go wrong. You are responsible for making tough and unpopular decisions. You often cannot share context that would build sympathy and understanding for you as a leader or the decisions you make in the company's best interest. It is reasonable to assume, then, that the individuals who can see leaders as people, and relate to them as such, are able to develop meaningful relationships that may ultimately advance their careers. For instance, how many people have the courage to invite their president or chief executive or manager to lunch? How many people have the courage to offer unsolicited advice or recommend a solution to a problem in the workplace? Sometimes we assume that if we are not close to others, they will not call on us for advice. But when you understand that people, regardless of their title, are just like you, you can speak with them in a way that affirms both your and their humanity. You can only do this if you keep fear in check.

I have thought for a long time about Leslie's advice, about my former colleague's willingness to be irreverent, and about what holds me back in the workplace. In relationships with managers, when I have been unafraid, I have been able to serve my boss and my company better because I speak the truth. Most managers appreciate authenticity and the ability to respectfully speak the truth.

How to Reduce Fear

To reduce fear, I recommend you make a list of everything that you're afraid of at work. Then make a list of what would happen if your fears came true. After that, write a contingency plan of what you would do if your fears came true, who you could lean upon for support, and what your strategy would be. Sometimes when we go through the process of listing our fears and making a plan of how we might respond, we realize that: (1) the chance of our fears coming to pass are slimmer than the mind would suggest, and (2) that we would survive even if our worst fears came true.

Next, to reduce fear in the workplace, take small, calculated risks that give you practice in speaking truthfully and appropriately to different colleagues. Roleplay with friends or family beforehand. Then choose people with whom there is minimal risk they'll respond aggressively. Practice speaking boldly with people you'd consider safe. The more practice you have, the more confident you'll become to speak more truthfully.

Finally, if you struggle with speaking up or speaking truthfully, think about the lessons you have learned growing up about communicating honestly. Was doing so safe, or were you penalized when you contributed your honest opinions? Sometimes it is not so much that our workplaces are unsafe but rather our conditioning around speaking honestly has convinced us that there are significant costs and repercussions for doing so. If you find yourself in such a position, counseling in this area may be helpful. I do not believe we are fundamentally different people at home than we are at work. If we behave a certain way in our personal lives and with our friends and family, we will often behave similarly at work. Therefore, it is important to consider why we behave the way we behave, think the way we think, and show up the way we show up.

What else can you do, or have you done, to name your fears and overcome them?

CHAPTER 10

We Are Fearfully and Wonderfully Made

A former boss of mine, former Ohio state senator I. Ray Miller, exudes confidence. Before joining the Ohio Senate, Mr. Miller was a member of the Ohio House of Representatives, a small-business owner, and the creator of legislation to establish a room in the Ohio Statehouse to honor the first African American legislator, George Washington Williams. He is now the publisher of a local newspaper. During the time when I worked with him, I observed a deep confidence. He believed in himself and his abilities, and that trust in self appeared to be unshakeable.

I wanted to know his secret to success and the source of his confidence, so I reached out to him. Senator Miller's response to my query about success and confidence shocked me. He told me that he "always walked into a meeting whole"—that he entered gatherings complete and settled within himself.

"I never thought anyone was better than me or that I didn't deserve to be there," he said. "I was sure of who I was and was committed to delivering an excellent product." His comments put me on my heels. How many times have I walked into meetings, grateful for the opportunity to be there but unsure that I had anything to contribute? How many times have I second-guessed my ability or waited for the validation of others? How many times have I been granted an opportunity based on my talent and skill, yet behaved as if I needed to continue proving my worth? More times than I care to admit.

Black women face a conundrum of needing to be confident in a world that doesn't always want or accept confident, assertive Black women. This is a contradiction that we will dodge from now until infinity. Yet there is something about learning to be confident and making a choice to showcase our confidence, regardless of whether people around us appreciate our doing so. And this confidence is not performative, but rather a natural state of being.

What I have come to learn from my work history and from watching people like Senator Miller is that racism, responsibility, and a myriad of experiences ensure that many of us are above average. There is no reason to shrink back. We are just as bright, capable, and witty as the people sitting next to us—just as smart as our colleagues and most certainly deserving of any opportunity that comes our way. What would it look like to fully own this awareness?

If my prodding has not inspired you to accept and own your brilliance, and you are a person of faith, perhaps a biblical text from Psalm 139:14—"I will praise you for I am fearfully and wonderfully made. Your works are wonderful.

I know that full well"—will do the trick. This Scripture is an affirmation that I was made with intention—that each of us was made with care and precision. Everything from my hips to the color of my skin to the texture of hair that adorns my head was specifically and intentionally made. Wherever I go professionally is where I am supposed to be, even if it is only for a season. I need not shrink in the presence of presumed greatness because I was fearfully and wonderfully made.

My Message to You

As a Black woman in a sometimes-hostile world, I want to remind you that you belong. As someone who has experienced being first and only, I want to remind you that the position you hold was tailor-made for your ingenuity, mode of thinking, presentation, and style.

When you find yourself feeling inadequate, try to trace the root of that emotion. For me, it was growing up with financial lack and growing up without both parents in the home. I know I had heard this Scripture more times than I could count, but I also know that I was ostensibly different from some of my family members and peers.

When you grow up with a lack of financial resources or financial stability, it is easy to fall into the trap of feeling like you are not enough because you don't have enough. This says nothing of racist ideals that undermine the worth and humanity of Black people in general and Black women in particular.

Let me share a couple examples to drive home how this belief in self plays out in the work world. If you believe you are not enough or that you do not belong, you may not fight for what you are clearly capable of doing. Early in my career in strategic communications, I was working on a labor matter and wanted desperately to handle the pitch to local media myself. I knew that the only way to learn was to do, and that learning by practical experience was key for some people. A consultant I was working with at the time told me and my boss that it would be better for him to handle the outreach to the media since he had relationships with the reporters in question. I pressed the consultant and my boss and convinced them that it was the issue, not the personality, that reporters cared about most; and if I had a compelling issue to share, reporters would listen. My boss agreed, and I was able to pitch the reporters in question.

I learned in that moment that while my Rolodex was not as deep as the consultant's, I was just as capable as he was. My abilities—to push back on what felt like an untruth about what it took to pitch reporters and speak up for myself— allowed me to learn and to do things that would advance my career down the line.

Your Perspective Is Valuable

Have you ever had an intuition that the approach your colleagues suggested was not the right one for the moment or situation the team was facing? Have you ever withheld your opinion only to watch things go up in flames? If so, you likely kicked yourself later for not having shared your thoughts sooner. You had a hunch that the approach was off key, but perhaps you didn't share that feedback because you lacked the courage and confidence to do so.

While I spoke up with the consultant, there were many times early in my career when I did not. I would sit in meetings and listen to problems and proposed solutions. My mind would be racing, but I sometimes lacked the confidence to share my perspective. Over time, I learned that my perspective was valuable. Yours is too.

Senator Miller once told me to never sit in a meeting and not contribute verbally. He told me to always make myself known. Now, when I am in situations and wondering whether my intuition is right and whether it makes sense to offer it, I remember Senator Miller's feedback. I realize that not only do I have a right to contribute, but everyone in the room has something to contribute. We are all as smart as the person to our left or right or in front or behind us. There is simply no reason to wait for or ask for permission to be our authentic, powerful selves.

Can you trace any sense of inadequacy you may have to its source? How have you learned the lesson of your own capabilities, and have you had a professional experience that underscores this lesson?

CHAPTER 11

Courage Sets Us Free

You cannot have a successful career without courage. You cannot have a worthwhile life without courage. Courage is not just speaking up when others remain silent. It is being willing to go to where no one in your circle has gone, to try what no one else around you has tried. It is making principled decisions, even when you are the first to make such decisions and even when those decisions could cost you dearly.

There is a reason Maya Angelou said that, of all the virtues, courage is the one that enables us to practice the others with conviction and consistency. One of the leaders I follow on social media is activist and author Hannah L. Drake. She has a direct and uncompromising style of challenging and highlighting injustice, and I admire her profusely.

As I mentioned in chapter 8, Hannah was working for the pastor of a church when another member of the staff hit her. When she confronted the church's pastor about the incident, he threatened to suspend her and made no attempt to rein in the other staff member or hold him accountable. Hannah was unwilling to be punished for being physically assaulted and quit her job. While she nursed a desire to be a writer, she had no leads for launching this career.

Yet she was confident that her calling was to write professionally and full time. While she was offered a new administrative job within weeks, she walked away from the opportunity to pursue a writing career. This took extreme courage. Today, Hannah has authored eleven books, is a sought-after public speaker, and is living the life she was called to live. Had she not demonstrated courage and righteous indignation, who knows when she would have accepted her calling of being a writer.

Courage Is a Necessity

When Robert F. Smith left an engineering job to go to business school and then into investment banking, his network of family and friends thought he had lost his mind. Then, when he opted to leave a lucrative career at Goldman Sachs on Wall Street to found Vista Equity, a private equity firm specializing in technology and finance, the people in his circle thought he was certifiable. He was blazing a trail that few before him had traveled or could envision. He likely had to draw from a reservoir of courage and self-assurance to go against the grain and lean into his heart's calling. But he did it. Today, he is wealthier than he likely ever could have imagined. He stunned the nation when he announced in spring 2019 that he would pay off the entire 2019 Morehouse College graduating class's student loans. I wonder whether he would have been able to do this had he not leaned into his passion and interests.

In the workplace, when you have an idea that upsets the usual way of getting things done, you will need courage and conviction to speak up and do what you know is right. When you observe colleagues or team members behaving in ways that threaten the organization or go against the desired culture, it will take courage to ensure that hard truths don't become unspoken truths. Courage is a necessity, not merely an aspiration affixed to motivational content.

If you are going to resist, you are going to need courage. If you are going to prioritize your own health and wellness, you will need courage. Why? Because Black women are expected to prioritize the needs of everyone else but ourselves. When you attempt to break out of this box, you are going to upset the apple cart, and you will receive criticism from women and men alike, and people from various races. To withstand and fight for yourself, you will need to be courageous.

What has been your experience with courage in the workplace?

PART IV

Strategies for Healing

CHAPTER 12

Get to Know Your Inner Child

"Take Our Daughters and Sons to Work Day" was designed to allow children and youth to explore career options. It's also an opportunity to see what their parents and caregivers do professionally. It's meant to be an educational experience for children and youth, and a chance to see how schoolwork connects to a myriad number of career fields. When children come to work, they are sure to lighten the mood with their youthful inquisitiveness and innocence.

But what happens when adults show up with their *inner child* in tow? There isn't a formal holiday for it, but it happens far more often that than you or I may realize.

Sometimes I show up well in work and social spaces. But more often than I care to admit, my inner child acts up. When my nine-year-old inner child shows up at work, I am usually surprised and baffled. My inner child doesn't trust easily. Experience has taught her that her opinions don't always matter, and that she is incapable of making her own choices.

She believes she has to say "yes" even when her insides scream "No!" At work, this manifests as saying "Yes, I can do it," when the appropriate response is, "No, I do not have the capacity to do that right now," or "Yes, I can do it—provided I have these supports."

My inner child doesn't navigate anger well because she was taught that anger is bad. Growing up, anger was met with judgment and labels, and the label was almost always "you're bad." At work, this manifests as the very thing that she doesn't want: losing her cool, failing to express what she does and does not like until it is too late, and tolerating inappropriate expressions of anger from others. I am clear that regardless of how much I've grown, my inner child tends to show up and does so at inappropriate times. I am clear that my success and my behavior are directly tied to the healing of my inner child.

My question for you is this: When was the last time you sat with your inner child? Is she well? Has she recovered from past hurts? Has she healed?

If your inner child is in perfect shape, you may want to skip to another chapter. If you think all is well with your inner child but you have relational problems at work and at home, please read on. And if you're questioning whether the notion of an "inner child" is real or child's play: well, keep reading.

Get Reacquainted

If you plan to lead people, or effectively lead yourself, you must get reacquainted with your inner child. Just because you are in young adulthood, middle age, or the golden years doesn't mean your inner child has caught up with your chronological age. If you experienced trauma as a child, your inner child may be stuck at the point or age of that trauma. Even if you walk around in a woman's size 10 shoe, your behavior may showcase an inner child who is much younger.

In *Trust: Mastering the Four Essential Trusts*, spiritual teacher and life coach Iyanla Vanzant writes:

> The psychological injuries and emotional wounds we experience as children affect our soul. When the soul does not develop within the experience of trust, there remains within us a child who is in a constant search for attention, understanding, love, respect, and possibly justice for her abuse or neglect. These needs, when left unmet and unaddressed, will fester and grow into disruptive and/or dysfunctional behavior patterns that will impact every aspect of our lives.

One of the ways I sense my inner child was showing up is that I can maturely resolve some issues in the workplace but come undone at the mere mention of others. More importantly, certain issues cause me to freeze up. When it came to coaching others on how to deal with being disparaged, talked about, and disrespected, I could easily rise to the occasion. But when I had to deal with colleagues who showed *me* disrespect, I would unravel. It was like I time traveled back to my childhood when I felt powerless or isolated based on factors outside of my control. Not only would I be unable to work through these and other conflicts alone; they would create such anxiety that I would engage in "fight or flight" mode. This created an adrenaline rush that was unsustainable for extended periods of time. When my inner child showed up, it was difficult for me to wrap my head around what I was feeling or communicate in a way that others understood. I was transported from the conference room right back to scenes from childhood.

The notion that our chronological age could be deceptive is rooted in research and commonly understood by therapists and those in the medical profession. "The fact is that the majority of so-called adults are not truly adults at all," writes Dr. Stephen A. Diamond in a *Psychology Today* article:

> We all get older. Anyone, with a little luck, can do that. But, psychologically speaking, this is not adulthood. True adulthood hinges on acknowledging, accepting, and taking responsibility for loving and parenting one's own inner child. For most adults, this never happens. Instead, their inner child has been denied, neglected, disparaged, abandoned or rejected. We are told by society to 'grow up,' putting childish things aside. To become adults, we've been taught that our inner child—representing our child-like capacity for innocence, wonder, awe, joy, sensitivity and playfulness—must be stifled, quarantined, or even killed. The inner child comprises and potentiates these positive qualities. But it also holds our accumulated childhood hurts, traumas, fears and angers.

Sometimes the clue that one's inner child needs some tending is conflict with someone *else's* inner child. I recall hiring a lovely woman to lead communications work. The woman had a gentle side and another side. She and I were like oil and water. We didn't mix. Despite our best efforts, we couldn't make it work. When I lamented this reality to my former therapist, she introduced me to this concept of our inner children conflicting with one another.

There are other ways that my inner child has shown up at the office. As a child, I worked desperately to please others. I took on too much responsibility, including the responsibility of going along to get along. When that tendency rears its head in the office, I ask myself whether the situation is triggering my inner child and whether that child has again taken over.

When was the last time you invited your inner child to dinner? When was the last time you watched her from afar? What did you observe? Was she happy? Did she relate to the world with enthusiasm, hesitance, or fear? Did she feel loved? What were her unmet needs?

These are questions you will need to know to understand your behavior and how to effectively relate to others.

After reading this section, what have you learned about your inner child? How do they show up in the workplace?

CHAPTER 13

Learn What's in Your House

In some instances, technical mastery guarantees success. When it comes to Black women, technical mastery, or knowing how to do the specifics of one's job, is the floor and not the ceiling for on-the-job advancement. It is like the entrance exam into law school: Doing well on the test will help you secure a seat in the program, but you need to clear a different set of hurdles to become a lawyer. To get and feel good in that dream job, Black women need to heal childhood wounds, challenge systemic racism, and adopt a lifestyle that prioritizes our personal care and nourishment. But we also need to be clear about the gifts we possess; the things we do effortlessly yet brilliantly; and the skills, forged through life experiences, that help us thrive. We need to be clear about what is in our house.

This phrase "what's in your house" is from 2 Kings 4:1–6 in the Hebrew Scriptures, or what many Christians call the Old Testament. This passage of Scripture highlights a newly widowed woman's complaints to the prophet Elisha. Creditors were harassing her and threatening to take everything she had, including her two sons, if she didn't satisfy her debt. How many of us can relate to being hounded by creditors, unsure of where to turn or how to come up with money to satisfy our obligations? Probably many of us.

Elisha responded by asking the woman, "What do you have in your house?" She told him all she had was a jar of oil. He told her to go borrow as many vessels from her neighbors as she could. She was to transfer oil from her jar into those vessels. This would enable her to pay her bills, Elisha told her. It turned out that with one jug of oil, she was able to fill all the vessels she had collected. Each time she poured out oil, it was replenished. In fact, she had more oil than she could use; she didn't have enough vessels to contain all the oil in her possession. She was then able to sell the oil for enough money to satisfy her creditors.

What's remarkable to me about this story is that the solution to the widow's problem was within her reach. Such is the case with us. For every problem we face, God has already provided a solution. Sometimes we have gifts that we undervalue or overlook because we don't see their worth. We don't look at the resources that are right inside our own house.

Some people were given the gift of words. They can communicate in a way that causes others to stop and listen. Think about some of the greatest orators of our time and the impact they have. I think about the Rev. Dr. William J. Barber II; when I hear him speak publicly, I am in awe. I think about Michael Render, aka "Killer Mike," and his command of history and language. Again, when I hear him speak, I never cease to be amazed. There is also the incomparable Nina Turner, an author, public speaker, Bernie Sanders 2020 national cochair, and former state senator from Ohio. While a political leader, she channels the spirit of a minister, and she can bring a crowd to their feet faster than the speed of light. These people are clearly gifted with oratorical skills.

Others of us have a passion for service. Our ability to care for others so they feel loved and appreciated can literally change lives. These are the people who run shelters, open their homes to people in need, and nurture and teach our children. My friend Teri Pritchett has this gift. Going to her home is like going to a bed and breakfast. Her hospitality is unmatched, and it is no wonder she has long worked with people experiencing homelessness.

For people blessed with the gift of courage, they can boldly call out injustice, and their vocal opposition can effect change. Others of us are mobilizers. We can mobilize people to action. We host a party or call a gathering, and people come. We launch an organization, and people line up to join.

The key is to never lose sight of what's in your house. Your liberation and the liberation of your people are influenced by not only what's in your proverbial house but also by your understanding of the gifts and skills that are uniquely yours. Regardless of what you face, you possess *something* that will help you overcome. It may seem like a small jar of oil to you, but it may just be enough. So, I must ask: What is in your house?

Let me share examples from my own family and life that illustrate what is in my house—both my personal house and the house of extended family members who raised me. I hope that these examples will help you assess what is in your house.

Faith and Service

One of my favorite experiences as a child was being at my grandmother's house and listening as my father, aunts, and uncles discussed the Bible. Their voices loud with assurance of their point, they would go over and over God's commandments. They'd debate why certain religious leaders were punished, what the apostle Paul meant when he wrote, "come out from among them, and be ye separate" (2 Corinthians 6:17) or what God intended to communicate with "Choose you this day whom ye will serve" (Joshua 24:15). This memory is so strong and favorable that even writing this gives me chills.

As important as they thought it was to study biblical texts, my family believed that Christianity was not confined to the walls of a congregation but that it must show up in community. Even though my parents divorced when I was four years old, my father remained an active parent. He was concerned about his own children and concerned about others' children as well. When my father picked up my siblings and me for visits, he'd sometimes pick up a neighbor's kids too. This neighbor was a white woman with seven or eight Black-biracial children. We all lived in subsidized housing, and my father must have worried about this woman raising so many children alone. He'd occasionally buy her children a shirt, pants, or dress right along with what he'd do for his own three children. My father's help for this neighbor was not an exception; he has lived much of his life helping others.

As I survey what's in my house, I also realize that service was a big component of my upbringing. My aunt Wanda would serve meals at the church she pastored and invite children from the neighborhood to eat. At Christmastime, she would buy toys for her children as well as children from the community. Other times, my father, my aunts, and my late uncle William would give or loan money to people in need. In other situations, they'd open their homes to people traveling through our city. They believed in service, and that service could be small acts, not just grandiose endeavors.

Writing

Another item in my house is the ability to communicate through the written word. I can write the way some people can run, effortlessly and quickly. This is a passion I discovered at a young age. In fact, since I was eleven years old, I have had a desire to write. This was a gift God gave to me, the worth of which I didn't always recognize. I didn't realize that my gift could matter. Writing is also one of the things for which people compliment me. When I was mired in debt, I prayed, and God reminded me that I could use the very gift God had given me—the gift of writing—to help me escape financial strain. After this revelation, I wrote my debut book, *Extraordinary PR, Ordinary Budget: A Strategy Guide*. Part of my liberation was within my reach.

Like me, you may become so accustomed to your own gifts that you think that they aren't a big deal. Maybe you aren't even aware you have them! But everyone has something to offer and something that someone else may need. There are no exceptions.

Why You Must Know What's in Your House

If you do not know what is in your house, you cannot develop a deep sense of self and an abiding confidence that will sustain you. If you do not know what is in your house, you will struggle with articulating your value and talents, particularly when it comes to negotiating in your best interest. If you do not know what is in your house, you may give away something that people are willing to buy. Understanding what gifts are unique to you, and what calling is uniquely yours, will set you up to not only advocate for yourself but also to believe in yourself, even when it appears no one else does. Knowing what's in your house is not just a nice thing to understand, it's an imperative for Black women. Too often we are undervalued and underappreciated. When you know what's in your house, you show up understanding your value without relying on the external validation that may or may not come.

This book focuses on the challenges Black women face being undervalued, unseen, and seldom celebrated. We cannot wait for others to discover our gifts, nor can we place our esteem in others' decision to celebrate us. We must take inventory of ourselves, understanding that we have value by virtue of existing. The gifts we have are merely icing on the cake.

What is in your house? Take a moment to think through the gifts you have that may help you. These may be resources from your background or individual talents. If you have a hard time thinking of anything, reflect on what friends and family notice that you're good at doing.

CHAPTER 14

Embrace Vulnerability

A painful and disorienting situation in my life was learning my son's father had married another woman. My son was a toddler at the time. In truth, my son's father and I had little in common and viewed the world differently: we weren't a good fit and never could have made each other happy. But that didn't stop my hope that he and I would be married. I desperately wanted to be married because I wanted my son to grow up with both parents and I wanted to avoid the stigma that comes with single parenthood. When word got to me that he had gotten married, and had done so without telling me, I was devastated. I cried so hard that when I called my friends to tell them what had happened, they could barely understand me through my tears.

Few times have I been as hurt as I was in that moment. My friend Theresa Todd could tell, and she immediately told me to pack a bag and come to her house. I remember this like it was yesterday. She lived on the campus of The Ohio

State University in a brownstone apartment building. She had two cats, and I despised cats, but even they couldn't keep me away. I was pitiful. Once I arrived, Theresa made me tea and listened to me pour my heart out. She allowed me to cry while assuring me that all would be well. She read to me from the Bible, played music for me, and created space for me to grieve. She allowed me to be vulnerable without judgment and without rushing me. When I left her apartment the next day, I had a little more hope than when I first arrived. She was a person with whom I was able to be vulnerable.

For centuries, Black women have been primed to be strong, matriarchal figures. We have been trained to care for everyone and to center everyone's needs but our own. This training is explicit and implicit. From an implicit standpoint, we watch the Black women in our lives and not enough of them have a practice of centering their own needs. The implied message becomes that we should center others. This shows up when our choices to do what makes us happy are undermined or questioned. Explicitly, we live in a racist and sexist society in which there are narrow expectations for Black women, and one of the prevailing expectations is to take on the matriarchal role, mothering as many people as possible. In all the explicit and implicit messages, there is seldom discussion around the importance of vulnerability and the limitations of the body.

Now, before I get into this chapter in depth, I need to acknowledge that while vulnerability is important, it is equally important to identify safe spaces where we can relax and share what is on our hearts and minds. Not all workplaces embrace vulnerability. Being vulnerable with the wrong person, at the wrong time, or in the wrong workplace, can have devastating consequences. One of the reasons nurturing strong relationships are so important is because those relationships afford us a safe space and room for vulnerability.

As Beulah Osueke, a Philadelphia-based communications strategist and youth basketball coach, noted to me:

> We are expected to be the backbones of our families and our communities, and we do not get breaks. Of course, this is amplified if a person is a natural leader. But Black women must be able to embrace vulnerability in a new way, and in a way that builds us up without causing us to question ourselves or feel any kind of guilt or shame. We need to begin teaching that acts of intentional vulnerability are a part of leadership development and not indicative of leadership regression.

Osueke is correct that leadership development should center vulnerability. The truth is that from childhood, many Black girls are taught that one day we will be wives, mothers, aunties, sister friends, and saviors. The key to being accepted in white spaces, and in many Black spaces, is to take on this otherworldly ability to care for others and to see and sympathize with the plight of others around us. To do this, we must feign strength. We must have the capacity and the desire to continually draw from a well of compassion, one that has been created and maintained for the benefit of others yet is bereft of resources for our own needs.

When Black women challenge this role and articulate a different vision for themselves, many are met with resistance and backlash. A Black woman with a career is told, "You are so busy; how will you ever have time for a man?" or "You need to put your children first." But is it really wrong to have a vision for your life that either doesn't include kids or a significant other? Is it really true that we cannot have aspirations and still be coupled?

Think about how often Black women come to the aid of others. Consider your own relationships. Are you the comforter, the consoler, the shoulder everyone cries on? Chances are that the answer is yes. In your relationships, how often are you permitted the benefit of vulnerability? And what would happen were you to display vulnerability?

In the workplace, Black women who care for others and singularly support the corporate vision, regardless of how troublesome its implementation may be, are rewarded. There are few spaces professionally or personally where vulnerability is permitted, let alone accepted or encouraged.

I recall going through a custody battle over my first child, who is now grown. His father and I eventually ended up in court. I was concerned about the negative aspersions cast on single parents—that we are fundamentally wrong, that we are irresponsible, that we are not enough. I was also so fearful of the damning labels assigned to women—that we are overly emotional and unstable—that I remained stoic throughout much of the harrowing proceeding. When I recounted in court what it was like to go through my pregnancy alone and without the support of my child's father, I didn't cry. When I recounted what it was like in the early days after my son's birth, as I struggled to find work and make ends meet, I spoke in an emotionless tone. I had learned to push my emotions so far down that I became numb; and on that day, I communicated from the head and not the heart.

After the court proceedings were over, my aunt shared that she believed my inability or refusal to show emotion during the trial had harmed me. When I talked about my hopes for the future, I tried to be as positive and upbeat as possible even though I was scared as hell. Even the process of going before a third party to convince them that I deserved custody of my only child was terrifying, yet I put on a brave face. Due to patriarchy, negative perceptions of women, and expectations that Black women be strong, I believed I could not show much emotion. It was hard to ask for help and to let people, other than a few close friends and family, know that I was in turmoil.

But in the words of Beulah Osueke: "People aren't taught to see Black women in their weakness." In fact, the inability to be vulnerable is harming us. We cannot hold in pain with no outlets for release without that taking a toll. An inability to be vulnerable can also cause us to overestimate our strength, abilities, and gifts. During a session at the 2019 Power Rising Summit, Linda Goler Blount, executive director of the Black Women's Health Imperative, shared that Black women do too much: "We take care of everyone but ourselves and we don't see ourselves and our health as broken or broke down . . . we work too much. We work almost 20 percent more than anyone else, and to no benefit."

What Is Holding Us Back from Being Vulnerable?

When Black women must constantly prove that we are good enough, smart enough, and talented enough to be in whatever room we are, there is limited space to show our vulnerability. And when we do, how have people responded? Think about it. If a Black woman who has held in trauma, pain, disappointment, or even happiness has a public display of anger, hurt, or exhilaration, how have others responded? With concern? With attempts to pathologize the person? And guess what—none of us are exempt from behaving poorly in the face of someone having a highly emotional reaction. Think about this the next time you experience someone who is angry, sad, or extremely happy. Sit with your first response. Ask yourself: Was my response judgmental or affirming? Ask yourself whether internalized racism has influenced your view of the situation and the person.

My broader point is that if we are not mindful, we will work ourselves into bad health trying to maintain a façade that all is well. Additionally, if we are not self-aware, we will respond to others in a way that reflects internalized racism. There must be space to acknowledge our own frailty and vulnerability, and we must always question why we do what we do.

How Can Black Women Demonstrate Vulnerability?

I recognize the seeming contradiction in my advice. On one hand, I am urging increased vulnerability by Black women. On the other hand, I am acknowledging that due to racism, sexism, and patriarchy, displays of need by Black women may not be well received. That shouldn't stop us from striving to be vulnerable, though. I think the key to doing this is resisting the norms that have been handed down to us about strength and vulnerability and forging ahead even when our vulnerability isn't readily received. This means that while everyone expects us to work, center the needs of others, and seldom take breaks, we must resist by resting. We must resist by saying, "No, I cannot help you with that right now," or "No, I cannot meet that need."

Several scholars and leaders have made this point. Academic and activist Rachel Cargle, in a published interview with EbonyJanice Moore for *Harper's Bazaar's* "Women Who Dare" series, agreed. Cargle noted that she wanted Black women to rest:

> Thinking of exhaustion also brings me back to my original question of us talking through what we do to fight back against systems, whether it's within ourselves, or our community, and it's never easy, but giving myself permission to rest. For a time, I felt that surviving as a black woman was my job. Not being a writer, not being able to develop meaningful stuff. And so resting, writing for fun, just writing a silly story, or just reading a novel instead of going through and feeling like I need to read every race book that's ever been written so I feel more equipped to exist in the world.

Cargle and Goler Blount underscore for me that if Black women are to survive and thrive and leave a healthier legacy for our daughters and nieces, we must rethink what it means to be a Black woman. We must be willing to do Black womanhood differently. Part of that means being vulnerable. It means centering our needs, even in the face of audible gasps and anger. Relatedly, I am making an intentional decision to share, within reasonable bounds, with the younger women in my life, such as my nieces, when I am not doing well or when I have failed. In fact, one time, when I was excluded from an event that I had made an extra effort to attend, I was disappointed and made a point of not hiding my sadness from my niece Ashante, who was with me at the time. I wanted her to see my imperfections. I wanted her to see me experience and work through disappointment. Part of this means being willing to say, "This hurt me," or "I am disappointed about X, Y, or Z."

Doing Black womanhood differently also means prioritizing our rest and walking away from the mandate that we keep producing and giving at all costs. During an interview with Glynda Carr, president and CEO of Higher Heights for America, a political organization for Black women, Carr summarized the need for self-care perfectly:

> We are at operation critical for Black women. The truth is, this is another year of my life that I am sleeping less, that I am less active. We can't continue to build a better life for our families if indeed we are not in it. We are suffering from major health challenges that include everything from heart attacks, to trouble having biological children to suicide. Many of our colleagues are taking their own lives because life felt like too much. I take stock of that. I am committing to checking in, and when I hear someone say something that seems off, taking time to actually unpack with the person what has been said.

Doing Black womanhood differently also means taking stock of our total health and then acting. Linda Goler Blount notes how negative stress not only contributes to ailments like diabetes and heart disease but also impacts how we metabolize food:

> Black women have about 15 percent more cortisol in their blood than white women. Cortisol changes the way we metabolize food. If you give black women and white women the same kind of diet, we [black women] gain weight faster. If you give black women and white women the same kind of low-fat diet, black women gain weight slower.

She went on to encourage Black women to write a list of all of their stressors and then a separate list of all the people who could help us, noting that "You are not in this alone and there is no reason for you to do this alone."

What Does It Look Like?

I had overcommitted myself again, having agreed to facilitate two retreats and an antiracism workshop for two different organizations in a two-day period. Before I even got to the sessions, I was stressed—not just because I wanted to perform well but because of everything it would take to show up and show up well. Our new puppy would need to be home alone for nine hours over two days. My daughter would need to be at daycare from 6:30 a.m. to 6:00 p.m. for at least one day of the training, something I tried to never do. Would I get caught in traffic? Would I need to pick up commuters so that I could use the express lanes into metro DC to get in and out of the city with ease (something that rarely happened)? It was no surprise that I had a stress headache in the days leading up to the trainings.

By day two of the training, I was willing to admit that I needed prayer. Reluctantly, and sheepishly, I asked the religious group for which I had just facilitated two meetings if they would say a word of prayer for me before I walked into my next training.

I will never forget what happened next. One enthusiastic organizer and executive director said, "Yes! I actually travel with an altar." She pulled out the makings of an altar—including a candle, a lighter, and a napkin to place the candle on—to create one right there in the center of our conference table. Another woman from the same organization said, "Yes, I came with blessed oil," and she proceeded to anoint me with frankincense. She poured the oil on her hands and then used those hands to put a cross on my neck. She then gave me custom prayer beads to wear around my neck. An older white woman jumped up and gave me two rubber bracelets. One bore the words, "You are enough. Don't ever give up." The other read, "You matter. Don't give up." The woman who gave me prayer beads led out in prayer, placing her hands on my head and praying for me with such intensity that I was moved to instant tears. When the prayer ended, another sister and executive director broke out in song. She then affirmed the light that was in me.

It was hard for me to leave that experience without breaking into an ugly, snot-flying cry. I did cry, but mostly I was grateful that I requested prayer and the group responded in kind. I left the experience more confident and more convinced that I was indeed loved. I walked into the other training feeling centered and assured of my purpose there. I like to think that how I showed up positively impacted the people in my subsequent training. Asking for and receiving prayer that day remains one of the oddest and yet most joyful experiences I have had. It was confirmation that vulnerability and prayer do in fact work.

Regardless of the expectations and blueprints handed down to us, Black women are not machines. We are living, breathing organisms with a finite amount of time, resources, and energy. We feel hurt like everyone else, and it is appropriate to express it in situationally appropriate ways.

Can you recount a time when you were vulnerable and you felt good about your decision to be vulnerable?

CHAPTER 15

Keep Work in the Proper Perspective

I am convinced that in America, too many people evaluate themselves based on the position they hold and the amount of money in their bank account. There have been so many times when my mood has been positively or negatively affected based on the balance in my checking account. Forget that I was healthy, that my children were healthy, or that we had a warm home, clothes to wear, and food to eat. All I could think about was how much money I had, how much money I needed, and what my possessions said about me as a woman, mother, and provider. I really should have been focused on my calling and life's work, but I was distracted. As Black women, we must set our affections on things that aren't always measured in dollars and cents.

I understand the desire and need to take care of ourselves and loved ones—believe me, I get it. But it is all too easy to base our worth on our careers. What's more, if we are not careful, we will judge others based on their career.

Further, sometimes we can look at people who are wealthy as though they are somehow better. We look at people who struggle financially as if they have made an insurmountable mistake—or worse, as if they have character flaws. No wonder then, that in many social settings, one of the first "break the ice" questions is, "What do you do?" Why does it matter what a person's profession is? Why aren't we questioning whether a person is a good human being, whether they are kind, whether they respect others? Why don't we value these things?

When the value of your life is so closely correlated with what you do, being terminated from your job can be devastating. Not only is there the fear of not being able to provide for oneself and one's family, which would be enough, there is also the blow to the ego and the challenging of a core part of our identity.

If we can prioritize *who* we want to be versus what we *do*, we will live more integrity-filled and intentional lives. If we focus on the calling that is uniquely ours or the work that we know we have been put on this earth to do, isn't it reasonable to conclude that we'd have greater peace and purpose?

When we focus on our character versus the rat race, we will make decisions that line up with the higher self we are working to cultivate and hone. This will affect all aspects of our lives—from the places we choose to work to the people we choose to engage. When we focus on who we want to become and what we are called to do, I believe that we can better cope with the challenges that will inevitably come.

When You Are Shown the Door

It's important to have proper perspective about who we are and what we are called to do because careers and external validation can be fleeting. You can be flying high one moment, enjoying acclaim and celebration, and be cast aside a moment later. No story brings home this point more powerfully than that of Bishop Carlton Pearson.

Bishop Pearson was a charismatic pastor, author, singer, host of the massively successful annual Azusa Conference, and an all-around influential leader in the Pentecostal church. He led a megachurch before the term was fully appreciated. Before there was a Bishop T. D. Jakes on the world stage, there was Bishop Pearson. He was a spiritual advisor to former president George W. Bush, and he counseled other presidents as well. But in the early 2000s, Bishop Pearson had a change in theology and announced that he no longer believed in hell. I don't know if there was something else happening behind the scenes, or whether this admission was the extent of the controversy. But once he articulated his changed belief system, Bishop Pearson lost everything. He lost his marriage, his church, his home, his friends, his savings, and even the rights to his name, which was apparently controlled by the organization he founded. The story is so profound that a film, *Come Sunday*, was made about his life. One of the reasons I was so moved by his experience is because I grew up listening to Carlton Pearson's songs, and I was comforted by his message as a young adult. It is difficult for me to wrap my head around how quickly life can change. How Bishop Pearson coped with losing everything remains a mystery to me.

There are other public falls from grace or public job terminations that invite exploration. Consider the singer and reality star Tamar Braxton and her removal from the daytime talk show *The Real*. Tamar had her own reality television show, *Tamar & Vince*, and starred in another reality show, *Braxton Family Values*, with her sisters. Despite the typical rumors via tabloids, Tamar appeared to be on top of the world. Her heavenly voice was beloved by fans. Her larger-than-life personality was consistently the source of conversation for entertainment reporters, fans, and foes alike. Her position on *The Real* was icing on the cake.

But in May 2016, just before the show entered its third season, Tamar abruptly departed *The Real*. Her removal was a surprise to fans, and many were heartbroken when they witnessed Braxton crying about the show's decision to let her go. There are a host of conflicting accounts about why the star lost the position, ranging from allegations that she had conflict with production staff to the idea that advertisers didn't want her in their commercials. Regardless of why she was let go, many people can empathize with being abruptly fired. And we can imagine how much more difficult this would be if one were a public figure. Scan your own career and perhaps you will be reminded of a time when you were shown the door—or perhaps showed someone else the door. Because since it's possible for all of us to be let go, downsized, or transitioned out, it is important to find a way to divorce our worth from our work. If we can remember why we are here and what we have been called to do, we may be able to see a glimmer of hope even in terminations. Additionally, each of us has a calling and purpose, and that purpose is larger than the roles we hold at any given moment.

I am focusing on job terminations and transitions in this chapter because it is something that most of us have experienced or will experience in the future. Even in perceived failure, we can be positioned to win. And sometimes what looks like failure is just realignment and repositioning for the future.

My broader point remains that our life's work and calling are bigger than the positions we hold. If we focus on who we are to become and what our purpose is in each moment, we will be grounded and better positioned for success.

If you have ever experienced a termination, how did you recover?

CHAPTER 16

Allow Others to Make Their Own Choices

Black women have enormous responsibility, but accepting responsibility for how people behave should not be one of them. This may seem counterintuitive depending on your career. In my career, I dole out professional advice as a publicist and consultant. When my clients do well, I am considered effective. But emotionally, I cannot base how I feel about myself on whether the people I work with do what I say. I care about each of my clients, and I want to see them to excel. Of course, it affirms my ego when my clients act on my recommendations and guidance. But should a client decide to disregard my counsel, I cannot take that personally. Neither should you.

If you are a parent, I am sure you know what I mean. We raise our kids and give them guidance that will help them excel. But at a certain age, they are responsible for their life and decisions. It is their life, and they will live with the consequences of their choices. If they decide a path for their lives that we disagree with, we must respect their decision, and—as my friend and spiritual coach Quanita Roberson says—"love them enough to let them stand in their choice."

What people do with the advice we share has more to do with them than it does with us. Our job is to tell the truth and to do so in a manner that works best for the recipient so that our message is received. Once we have told the truth and offered the best advice possible based on our understanding of the situation, our job is complete. We should not take on the responsibility of controlling the outcome. This is entirely too much pressure, and it sets us up to fail.

Moreover, the ego has an insatiable appetite. It demands to be extolled, to be fed, and to be obeyed. Even the meek among us, if not careful, may yield to its demands. The more accomplished or educated people become, the more susceptible they may be to expect others will act on their advice. I have learned that the ego, coupled with expertise, can be a potent—dare I say toxic—mix.

It makes sense. When one has achieved a certain level of success, the ego can take on a persona of its own. That persona wants allegiance from all in its employ. But getting someone to behave the way we want is entirely too heavy a burden to bear.

Advise and Recommend

Regardless of how much we have accomplished or how smart we are, we cannot force our will on another; nor can we make people do what they do not want to do. Quite simply, our job is to offer candid advice and to recommend the best course of action to the people with whom we work. I know we all feel passionately about our experience, gifts, and skill sets. However, the danger grows when we become angry because others will not act on what we have advised or when we feel responsible for a person's poor choices.

I am a smart person. I think things through and look at problems from multiple vantage points. By the time I make a recommendation, I am usually confident it is the right thing to do. But in the end, my worth is not diminished because others refuse to act on my advice. What matters is not my ability to coerce others to do what I say but whether I have offered the best advice possible given the information available at the time.

When was the last time you advised or recommended a colleague or boss do something that the individual did not want to do? How did it make you feel?

CHAPTER 17

Choose Empathy over Performance

This chapter could literally be called "Confessions of a Reformed Bad Boss." My intention is to be brutally honest about a lesson it took me years to learn.

For years, I prioritized work over people. I wanted the work to get done regardless of how it was done or who I had to sacrifice to complete the task at hand. I was so desperate to please the higher ups, and so mired in my own quest for perfection, that I held myself and everyone around me to impossible standards. I would get so riled up about a work project that I would overemphasize its importance and devalue the person who was actually completing the project or the coworkers I was supervising.

This is an orientation toward work and a habit to which I've grown accustomed. Breaking this pattern requires attention and intention. Sadly, at points in my career, I became so obsessed with delivering a stellar product that I lost sight of the people helping to ensure the product's completion. If colleagues didn't cut it—if they couldn't deliver in the way I had hoped—I had little regard for them.

If Black women are to thrive at work, I believe we must do more to honor our own humanity and that of others. I have come to appreciate that all people are worthy of love, respect, and dignity. Regardless of their performance or their ability to do the job they were hired to do, all people have inherent value. Everyone deserves appreciation and respect. If they are unable to do the job for which they have been hired, their manager must either coach them up or transition them out. Even if you must transition a team member out of their role, it's important to do so while honoring their humanity. Focus on the work product and not the person, and be clear that just because things didn't work out doesn't mean that they do not have value. In some cases, offering a severance can also assist with the transition process.

To be clear, I do not believe that anyone sets out to harm others at work. Focusing on the bottom line, at the expense of the very people who help us reach the bottom line, is a consequence of capitalism. Capitalism places a premium on work, work products, and output. It couldn't care less about a person's humanity and narrowly focuses on what a person can do. When one person ceases to perform, capitalism mandates that another person be put in their place. Many of us are rewarded when we relentlessly produce. We are rewarded with raises and promotions, which can equate to more work and more responsibility. We are rewarded with status and social capital.

Even if the reward isn't financial, being well regarded and liked is affirmation in and of itself. For those primed to be people-pleasers, being well spoken of is important. We tie our identity to the work we do and believe that the more we accomplish, the harder we work, the more money in our bank accounts, the more value we have.

But work is what we do; it isn't who we *are*. It is easy to obsess over output, performance, and productivity and miss the beauty in the people around us. I wish someone had reminded me early in my career that the people I worked with and for had value that was bigger than the temporary roles they played in the organizations we worked for or what they could produce.

To truly see the humanity in others, you must recognize the limitations of capitalism. You must also recognize your own limitations and your tendency to make judgments. Sometimes when we judge others too harshly and obsess over their output, it's because we are also judging ourselves too harshly. For instance, if you are loving and generous with yourself, it becomes easier to be loving and gentle with others. But if you look at yourself from a place of deficit, that is the lens through which you see the world. If you have a practice of judging yourself, you will indeed judge others. When you can look at yourself and choose context over judgment, you can do the same for others. But it is a mistake to think that we can somehow treat others better than the way we treat ourselves.

Most of us have a to-do list a mile long and believe that we have the capacity to do everything on that list—even though our health, relationships, and mental well-being suffer in the process. We overestimate our abilities and over-burden our minds and bodies. Part of this stems from our acceptance of the "Black women as superwomen" myth; part of this comes from how we are used to operating in our families of origin; and part of this is resignation in the face of systems of patriarchy, sexism, and racism. Some of us, myself included, are accustomed to carrying so much pressure and responsibility that we begin to volunteer for it. If our work lives seem slow, we take on a new project. In meetings, we are the first to raise our hands when our colleagues request help. If we have space in our workday, we either fill the time or beat ourselves up for being slothful. None of this acknowledges our frailty or humanity.

Until we can break this pattern and see our own humanity, limitations and all, we will be less likely to see and honor the humanity in others. And we will be less healthy in the process.

How to Do It

Regardless of people's performance or the leadership role they play, everyone needs empathy. A fancy title, a big office, or the ability to call the shots doesn't eradicate a person's humanity. An inability to perform to the expectations of others is also not justification to treat a person poorly.

To see the humanity in others, we must see our own humanity. We must understand and embrace our limitations. We cannot give to others what we do not have for ourselves. We cannot show up for others when we're unable to show up for ourselves. The next time you feel tempted to judge yourself, give yourself love instead. Acknowledge mistakes, sure. But then acknowledge that you tried and for that, you have something to celebrate.

To see the humanity in others, we must cultivate empathy. Empathy is the ability to understand, anticipate, and share in another's feelings. It is a powerful skill that allows others to feel seen, heard, and valued. It is also a critical factor in healthy work environments. In an article for *Forbes*, Tracy Brower notes that empathy "facilitates cooperation, which is critical for teams to function effectively." She cites research showing that "when empathy was introduced into decision-making, it increased cooperation and even caused people to be more empathetic. Empathy fostered more empathy." To cultivate empathy, you must be in proximity with colleagues. Get to know them on a personal level and learn about their upbringing and life. As you learn about people, you gain context on their story and history. This context enables you to have more empathy.

Here's an example. I was going through a tremendously tough time at work and at home. Professionally, I was managing transitions on my team and budgetary challenges. I needed to make a series of difficult decisions and then announce those decisions to staff. Personally, I was navigating being a single mom of a toddler while offering emotional and financial support to an older child who was incarcerated. During a particularly stressful meeting, during which I needed to announce that we couldn't fill an open position, a staff member not only listened intently but ended the conversation by telling me that she supported me and would help in any way necessary.

A few hours after the meeting, she checked in with me to inquire if I was personally doing okay. I was speechless. Literally speechless. Transitions are hard for everyone. No one likes organizational change that may mean more work for them or a change of one's portfolio, as this one did. It would be natural and understandable to focus exclusively on how change impacts you. For the employee to step outside of her situation and inquire about *me*—the supervisor who was initiating the change—really blew my mind. This employee's ability to express empathy was not a one-off situation but rather a consistent character trait.

If you are struggling with seeing the humanity of colleagues, cultivate empathy. Not only will doing so help the individual; it will also help the team. To do this, try getting to know people outside of their professional role or title. As you think about how they impact your life, follow up by asking how their life has been impacted and by whom. When you feel critical or judgmental, ask yourself how you would want others to respond if the roles were reversed.

Reflect on a time that you acknowledged someone else's humanity or when someone else acknowledged yours. How did both scenarios feel? What did you learn?

CHAPTER 18

Communicate with Care

You are always communicating, even when your lips are sealed. You are always sending messages. And trust me: someone is always watching. My question to you, oh fierce Black woman, is this: What are you communicating?

I'd like you to try an experiment. If your office has a see-through or glass conference room, sit outside of it right before a meeting. Watch your colleagues as they head into the meeting, and then develop a narrative for each attendee. If you do not work in an office, during a remote video conference with colleagues or during a face-to-face meetup, pay attention to what people are communicating nonverbally. Then assess what you have learned.

Whether you realize it or not, you are always communicating. Each time you walk into your office, walk into a meeting, sit with colleagues, or do something as natural as eating lunch, you are communicating something. In addition to listening to what is verbally communicated, your manager and colleagues will pay attention to what is unspoken.

If, in a meeting, you cut everyone in the room off when they're speaking, you communicate that you believe what you have to say is more important than others' contributions. If you optimistically respond to the recommendations of others, you are communicating openness and welcome. If you are clear about your capacity and voice that to colleagues, you are communicating that boundaries are important and valuable to you.

As you navigate work and life, think about the message you are communicating and the message you'd *like* to communicate. What do your actions and presence communicate about you? How intentional are you in monitoring what you convey?

Control Your Narrative

You can do a variety of things to be more mindful of the messages you are sending. You can use language that you hope others will use about you. For instance, when I work with leaders in a professional capacity, I ask them how they want to be recognized or known in the world. I encourage them to think about what they want. Once they are clear about how they want to be recognized, I ask them to include that language in their bios, in their communication, and in their social media profiles. I ask them to call themselves what they want others to call them. Put out in the world how you want to be known, rather than letting others control your narrative.

When you criticize others' suggestions and repeatedly find fault, you are either in the wrong work environment or critical by nature. None of this makes you a bad person, but it may explain why people either come to you for guidance or shy away from you.

People are listening to what you say, how you say it, and what's left unsaid. It may take time for the data to be compiled, but in time, a full picture will emerge because you are always communicating. As we navigate different work environments, we should assess what we are communicating and whether that message is the one we intend to convey.

As you assess your life, think about what you have been communicating. Are you comfortable with that message? If not, what do you want to change?

PART V

Paths to Liberation

CHAPTER 19

Understand Which Force You Are Fighting

Racism, sexism, economic uncertainty, homophobia, childhood trauma, familial stress: Black women must contend with a variety of forces. It is imperative we know on which plane we are fighting. We cannot precisely direct our prayers, marshal the correct resources, or understand our role in a situation if we do not understand what battle we are fighting at any given time. This is not to say that we will not face simultaneous challenges. We can, and often do. But if we can name them, it is easier to name the corresponding help we may need to overcome those challenges. We cannot give ourselves the love we require if we do not appreciate the extent of the challenges before us. If we do not understand on which plane we are fighting or appreciate the difficulty of the terrain we are encountering, we will burden ourselves with the responsibility to solve something that we didn't create and that we may not have the power to solve on our own.

When we think about what it takes to thrive as the first and only, we must be clear about what is ours to carry and what belongs to others. In addition to knowing how to do our jobs, we must also appreciate the difficulty—and necessity— of performing while contending with racism, sexism, sexual harassment, personal trauma, or familial troubles.

Isn't It Enough to Simply Work Hard?

When I was younger, I thought the key to professional success was working hard and doing a good job. I vowed to keep my head down and outwork everyone around me. It took years for me to learn that my assumption—that hard work is the only prerequisite for on-the-job success—was sophomoric and naive. Of course, hard work is important, but for Black women, that is just the first step. Hard work won't prepare us for the toll of racism, sexism, homophobia, ageism, and other barriers. These things are always present, and they affect our ability to perform well. Further, even when we check all the boxes and do everything right, there is still work that must be done externally to ensure we get the opportunities that we deserve.

We must start with an understanding that Black women battle on multiple terrains, and we often do so simultaneously. For instance, we are navigating what it means to be the first and only in many work and professional settings. We are navigating how to work and thrive in non-Black spaces and, sometimes, in anti-Black spaces. We are negotiating how to balance our feminine and masculine energy: part of this is thinking through and practicing how to assert our value and boldly advocate for our self-interests. We are navigating how to work hard yet still show up consistently and presently for our families. If we are the heads or breadwinners of our households, we understand that being present while saddled with responsibility for how our families will thrive financially is an especially unique and draining task. Those of us who are trauma survivors may judge our experiences through the lens of our previous traumas while still trying to show up and perform as expected and required. This says nothing of the struggles that accompany mere existence: health and mental health challenges, familial strain, financial issues, and domestic violence.

In addition to what I have outlined above, Black women must also push back against judgments on our appearance, hairstyles, skin hue and tone, communication style, background, and professional presentation. Since whiteness is the standard for beauty in this nation, Black women are constantly evaluated based on our proximity to it.

With this as the backdrop, Black women are often expected to be exceptional at work yet are penalized when we are. The reason I say we are expected to be exceptional is because throughout our careers, we hear so much negative feedback, often colored by gender and race—about everything from our person to our work style to our interpersonal relationships—that we begin to chase perfection. We chase perfection to silence the critics. Of course, perfection is not possible, but we are tired of being criticized or told that, if we change this one little thing, we'll find success.

Yet the flip side of perfection or excellence is white resentment. A Black woman can go from being beloved to being threatening in a space of weeks, if not days. Attorney Erika Stallings writes that this phenomenon "happens when women, typically Black women, are embraced and groomed by organizations until they start demonstrating high levels of confidence and excel in their role, a transition that may be perceived as threatening by employers."

If you are reading this book as a non-Black woman, and this is beginning to feel impossible or tiring, I hope you will think carefully about the hurdles you force Black women to clear and change your behavior. If you are not actively a part of the solution, you are contributing to the problem. If you are reading this as a Black woman, I hope you will see that it is not you, it is them. Be affirmed in knowing that countless other Black women are experiencing what you are experiencing.

My main point is this: it is imperative that Black women understand that we are contending with a lot of forces. When we succeed, it is often against the odds. This is cause for celebration and a relaxing of the rules in terms of what counts as success. In some cases, simply surviving in anti-Black spaces is victory. Recognizing one's inability to manage the emotional labor of surviving in such spaces is also cause for affirmation and applause. But when we cannot survive, it is definitely okay to plan our escape and walk away. We must measure ourselves using our own rubric, not the one passed down by colonialism, racism, and sexism.

As I have said elsewhere in this book, technical mastery is not a panacea for professional success. There is the spiritual, emotional, and physical cost of showing up as the first and only. To the extent we can recognize this, grieve this, and then adapt strategies to support us, we will be much happier.

When it seems like you are confronted with multiple challenges at once, what have you done to support yourself?

CHAPTER 20

Resist the Good-Bad Binary

Black women are often given two options. If you want to be accepted, you must be "good," which means putting the comfort and pleasure of others above your own. If you decide that autonomy and freedom of thought are principles that all people, including Black women, should embrace, you could be labeled "bad." When Black women accept cues to be good, we choose to remain quiet even when our survival necessitates we speak. Being good means self-denial. If you have a vision for your life that centers your wants and desires, you could be labeled bad. If you ruffle the feathers of the people around you, arousing their fear, scorn, or skepticism, you will be labeled bad. If you have the temerity to display anger or discuss your experience with anger, you may again be labeled bad.

The labels show up when leaders prop up one person, the agreeable one, and put down another. These labels show up when companies and leaders create categories of "good" and "bad" (or "problem") employees. These labels can even show up in our psyches without intentionality, awareness, or work.

Yet Black women must be aware that this dynamic exists, even as we work to embrace all aspects of ourselves. The people who manage us and interact with us must also be aware of this dynamic.

In a February 2019 TED Talk, Soraya Chemaly, author of *Rage Becomes Her: The Power of Women's Anger*, notes that "When we say what is important to us, which is what anger is conveying, people are more likely to get angry at us for being angry." When Black women communicate that a boundary has been crossed or that a need is not being met, many people focus too much on how they express this feedback versus the message they are intending to convey. In these situations, it is all too easy for us to be labeled "bad" or even scary.

"Anger confirms masculinity and it confounds femininity," Chemaly adds, noting that "men are rewarded for displaying it and women penalized for doing the same." I wholeheartedly agree and would add that, in addition to anger being gendered, the "angry Black woman" stereotype means that finding space to express anger can be tricky. Even with thought leadership such as Chemaly's book, people still struggle with seeing Black women in the fullness of our humanity. Part of being human is having emotions; and anger, just like other emotions that healthy humans display, is a valid and necessary one.

But the pressure for Black women to opt to be "good" in order to be accepted is enormous. Again, being good looks like shunning anger, accepting anything and everything that comes our way, tolerating abuse and harmful relationships, refusing to demand appropriate compensation, and refusing to voice dissent or an opposing viewpoint. In this posture, we do what we're asked without complaining and without an expectation of reciprocity, justice, or fairness. When we're paid less than our white or male counterparts, for instance, a "good" Black woman is just grateful to have a job. A "good" Black woman is a superwoman, shouldering more than her fair share of responsibility and yet lacking the resources to truly do a good job. Further, "good" Black women are benevolent supporters of others, decentering themselves in the process.

As writer Najma Sharif points out, "Black women are offered crumbs and are expected to be grateful for it all while being in service of everyone but ourselves. And we have to do it with a smile. How cruel. I don't have it in me to rant about this so it's time to go cry."

On the other side of the coin is "bad." The Black woman who is labeled this way has an opinion and isn't afraid to share it. When her boundaries are crossed, she may display anger, which is an internal warning that her needs are not being met. Yet this reaction can simultaneously provoke labels of crazy, angry, and unreasonable.

If she believes that justice and equality apply regardless of race, gender, or sexual orientation, her reasonable belief in her right to equity annoys others. If she is vocal in her pursuit of getting what she feels she deserves, she may rankle the people around her in the process. She is known as "not nice," "bad," "mouthy," and perhaps "an angry Black woman." Sure, some colleagues will tell her in private that they appreciate her voice, but it rare for them to stand with her in public.

What Black Girls Face

This conditioning starts when girls are young. Not only are girls not permitted to be angry; they are punished for it. In 2019 in Orlando, Florida, officer Dennis Turner arrested a six-year-old Black girl for doing what many six-year-olds do: throwing a temper tantrum. She was placed in handcuffs and given a juvenile case number. Sadly, she was not the first young Black girl arrested in school. In 2005, St. Petersburg, Florida, police arrested five-year-old Ja'eisha Scott at her Pinellas County school. I can't think of a louder way to tell a little girl to be good than placing her in handcuffs.

Clearly, messages about acceptable behavior are sent from childhood into the teen years and eventually into adulthood. Jasmine Tucker, director of research at the National Women's Law Center, summarized the unique challenges Black girls face for *The Independent*, noting that "black girls face assumptions about 'who they are and what they are like' built on stereotypes."

Sadly, respectability politics and the pressure to be "good" doesn't go away as we age. In everyday life and in most interactions, we must calculate when we speak up, how we speak up, whether we are nice when we do, and a host of other factors that are just tiring. What's more, even suppressing anger doesn't keep us safe. Think about the Duchess of Sussex. From the time of her engagement through to her marriage and the birth of her son, Archie, life has been anything but problem-free for Meghan Markle. She has been subjected to the verbal taunts of an estranged father and a mean-spirited stepsister who has seemed intent on ruining her life. In reference to her treatment by British tabloids, many outlets, including The Guardian, noted that "Meghan appeared close to tears as she spoke of coping with the pressure, particularly after the birth of their first child, Archie. 'It's a very real thing to be going through behind the scenes,' she said. 'The biggest thing that I know is that I never thought it would be easy, but I thought it would be fair. And that's the part that's really hard to reconcile.'"

Meghan may be royalty, but she is still a Black woman. I, like many other Black women, claims her as sister. We understand that by sheer virtue of her race, gender, and culture, she will always navigate several intersecting identities. She has a privilege that many of us will never know, and yet that privilege will not shield her from racism, sexism, or xenophobia. I mention xenophobia because I am not clear what portion of the harassment she receives is based on her identity as an American and which is based on her identity a biracial Black woman. Regardless of the root of scorn, the fruit is painful.

Further, our professional spaces often push Black women to the edge and then colleagues or supervisors feign surprise when we snap. Melissa Harris-Perry's very public exit in 2016 from MSNBC is case in point. Harris-Perry had a phenomenal show on the network. Movement leaders, people who led grassroots groups and campaigns, felt her show was the place to shine a light on injustice. They found in Harris-Perry not just an ally but a coconspirator in the fight for justice. Naturally, when she stopped hosting her show and then wrote an impassioned letter to her staff where she said she would not be a token, fans and viewers wondered what had happened. Whatever went down at MSNBC, Harris-Perry was having none of it. She wrote a sharply worded letter to her colleagues and publicly announced that she was not a token and would not be used. As a PR person, I have been trained to protect the brand at all costs, so Harris-Perry's exit was surprising. I knew that she must have been profoundly hurt to release such a candid and unscripted letter.

Sexuality

Up to this point, I've focused on the workplace, but the good-bad dynamic shows up in how we embrace and display our sexuality as well. Black women who embrace their sexuality and sexual energy are sometimes held out as objects of derision. Should a Black woman have sexual agency and express an interest in sex outside of reproduction, she is oversexualized or chastised by the respectability police and various religions. In *Passionate and Pious*, author Monique Moultrie examines the impact of the Black Christian church, faith-based sexuality ministries, and religious media on Black women's sexual agency and sexual decisions. She notes that "many black churches are willing to pay attention to women's sexuality as long as it is to impugn black women's sexuality as an evil that needs to be controlled."

Further, Black women, like all women, are subject to continual messages about our weight, physical appearance, and personal grooming. Such cues can easily lapse into shaming when we are outside the norm of the fashion and beauty industry. But as author and body positivity champion Sonya Renee Taylor has said, "the body is not an apology."

We should continually strive to experience the full range of emotions even as we defy and abandon the good versus bad binary. To place this binary aside requires our collective participation. I'm in. Are you?

When have you been labeled "good" and "bad?" How did those labels impact you?

CHAPTER 21

Keep Asking for What You Need—Despite Resistance

Most leadership books urge women to advocate for ourselves. Katty Kay and Claire Shipman's book *Confidence Code*, for example, urges women not to wait for perfection before putting forth a new idea, and not to wait until yearly reviews to request a salary increase. They suggest that a contributing factor to the wage gap between men and women is women not asking, or not asking as frequently, for wage increases. While this is great advice, their book and many other leadership books do not talk about the penalty that can be levied against Black women when we do speak up and make our preferences known.

The truth is that Black women who ask for what they want and need are not always greeted with celebration or applause. Our requests are analyzed through the lens of race, gender, socioeconomic realities, and a host of other factors. Consequently, what may be a reasonable request for a white woman or a non-Black person of color can be considered inappropriate when posited by a Black woman. The penalties we experience for asking for what we want can be anything from being labeled "difficult," "uppity," "presumptuous," or "arrogant," to facing snide remarks, gaslighting, or retaliation.

Asking for what you want and need could look like asking for a modified work schedule—one that meets your and your family's needs. It could look like pushing your doctor to do one more round of testing when you know something is off in your body. Perhaps it's advocating for something your child needs at school. Other examples include advocating for diversity in the workplace, asking for a raise, or making a request for how you want other people to treat you. All these very necessary requests can be met with backlash for Black women.

Time and again, research has shown that racial diversity, diversity of perspective, and diversity of experience and background all benefit organizations and companies. Most people, including most leaders, claim to value diversity, right? Unfortunately, Black women and people of color are often penalized for championing it.

A study on what researchers called "diversity-valuing behaviors"—such as "whether they respected cultural, religious, gender, and racial differences, valued working with a diverse group of people, and felt comfortable managing people from different racial or cultural backgrounds"—found disturbing evidence that advocating for diversity can disadvantage one in the workplace. This research team found that "women and nonwhite executives who were reported as frequently engaging in diversity-valuing behaviors were rated much *worse* by their bosses, in terms of competence and performance ratings, than their female and nonwhite counterparts who did not actively promote balance." Further, white male executives do not receive career benefits for pushing diversity, and nonwhite and female executives are often actually punished for doing so. This study, which included 350 executives, was published in the *Academy of Management Journal* in 2016.

What is particularly disturbing is the way Black women and Black people in general can be placated during our attempts to push diversity. The message white people share with Black people in public is often quite different from what they share with other white people in private. I will never forget working in the Ohio Senate and having a colleague who was an affable Italian man. He was super friendly and always had a smile on his face. Years after I left the experience, a white friend told me how horribly this guy spoke about Black people. Had she not told me, I never would have guessed the level of anti-Blackness and racism he harbored internally.

Advocating for Yourself

A similar dynamic exists when it comes to salaries. When Black women have the temerity to ask for increased wages and better benefits, they can face penalties for doing so. Hannah Riley Bowles, a senior lecturer at Harvard's Kennedy School of Government and the director of the Women and Power program, has studied gender effects on negotiation through laboratory studies, case studies, and extensive interviews with executives and employees in diverse fields. In a story for the *New Yorker*, journalist Maria Konnikova noted that Bowles has "repeatedly found evidence that our implicit gender perceptions mean that the advice that women stand up for themselves and assert their position strongly in negotiations may not have the intended effect. It may even backfire."

So, leadership books that present a one-size fits all approach to self-advocacy do Black women and women a disservice. We face unique barriers, and the leadership class must be better at pointing that out. None of this is to say that we shouldn't advocate for ourselves, but we should be prepared to face backlash when we do, and we should be equipped with strategies for navigating such terrain. For instance, it is a good idea to identify advocates inside the workplace who can advocate for us, even as we are advocating for ourselves. To do this, we must understand who the power brokers are, cultivate meaningful relationships across the organization, and be honest about our need for allies and partners. I am also not above explicitly asking for advocacy help from trusted colleagues. When I join an organization, I am on a quest to identify my allies and potential allies.

Why does this matter? In four studies, Bowles and collaborators from Carnegie Mellon found that "people penalized women who initiated negotiations for higher compensation more than they did men."

And to be clear, the penalties don't have to be leveled for things as big as championing diversity or asking a raise. We can experience penalties when we insist that our voice is just as heard as non-Black women's voices in meetings, or when we take up space. We can be penalized for having confidence. We can also be penalized if we are too good at our jobs, and therefore considered a threat. Yes, that's a thing too.

If you couple this with the fact that Black women have long been confronted with the "angry Black woman" stereotype, navigating the penalties associated with asking for what we want and need can be tricky. In particular, this stereotype requires making calculated decisions around how one raises dissent, how one responds to aggression, how one handles attacks, and how one advocates for herself. Even when a Black woman has justifiable reasons for anger or concern, the "angry Black woman" trope can cause others to focus on our expression instead of the underlying problem. Internally, it can cause Black women to second-guess ourselves or become passive or fearful.

Niceness Is a Construct

And since we're speaking of passivity—I'm convinced that America wants passive, toe-the-line women in general and Black women in particular: women who are content to live in the shadow of others and willing to dispense with any thought of what we rightfully deserve or desire. Black women are often asked to discard any notion of fairness and justice in the workplace and often in life. If we attempt to press charges against our non-Black abuser, the police may question if this is really the approach we want to take. If we question mistreatment in the workplace, as I did when a colleague complained that I was using my pregnancy to get special treatment, we are sometimes reminded of how awesome the offender is despite their offense. When Black women have the audacity to show up, ask up, and live up to our highest vision for ourselves, doing so may rankle the people around us. We should do it anyway. Even if no one else does it, we should commit to standing with and for ourselves.

If you are someone who can ask for what you want or need without regard to what others think, I applaud you. Doing so requires a level of confidence, assertiveness, and belief that it is okay to take up space. Asking for what you want and need requires an underlying belief that your needs will be met. If you are someone who struggles in this area, consider thinking of yourself as your own protector. As protector of yourself, it is your responsibility to self-advocate. Name the side of you that serves as a protector and enlist that side to boldly request what you need.

In case it is not apparent, what I am describing is bigger than knowing how to ask or asking nicely. "Niceness" is a construct that was created to uphold privilege and power. Niceness is also subjective and interpreted through the lens of one's background and culture. You can be as polite as Mother Teresa, but if a person has a problem with your mere existence, and if they are fundamentally anti-Black, they will find a way to dismiss, critique, or label you. In this instance, there is nothing you can do to be acceptable to them, nor should you seek their validation or approval.

Again, I am not sharing this to prevent you from asking for what you want and need. I am sharing this so that you know that you won't always be met with a welcome mat.

Forge ahead anyway. We should view every piece of advice through a racial and gender lens, then make a plan that takes race, gender, and gender identity into account.

What penalties have been levied against you when you have asked for what you needed, and how did you respond in the face of them?

CHAPTER 22

Seek Counsel from Black Women and Allies

I remember musing to my colleagues once that it would be amazing to attend the Sundance Film Festival. I wanted to simply attend, but when I voiced this idea to my team members, one of them, Chelsea Fuller, responded, "Maybe we can host a panel or reception for a film that aligns with our work." In an instant, my idea was upgraded. We went with Chelsea's idea and she took the lead on finding a film. We landed on a biopic about Aretha Franklin, *Amazing Grace,* and she coordinated with the film's producers so that the racial justice organization for which I worked, Advancement Project, could host a reception for it.

Over time, I have learned that I can come up with an idea. I can develop amazing plans. Yet those plans are sometimes improved when shared with others. In many situations, what I once considered a good idea blossoms into a great one after I have shared it with others. Having the right people around you, and the courage to ask for input, can dramatically improve the initial product or idea.

In other situations, ideas that I thought made a lot of sense were sidelined after I sought input. There have been times when I haven't had the context or perspective to understand how different groups might perceive various actions. The beauty of counsel is that you test-run ideas and determine if they make sense.

There is something beneficial about distance. Sometimes we are so close to an issue that we are unable to see what others can. That is one of the reasons it is so important to be proactive about seeking counsel. While this is important for all people, it is critical for Black women.

Given the challenges Black women face—pay disparities, income inequality, discrimination over our hair and bodies, the list goes on—we must have allies, and we must be in community with each other. We need women who are on or who have been on the same path as we are, and who can understand the challenges we face. We need people for whom we do not have to translate what it means to be Black and female. Additionally, there is value in having culturally aware allies who represent different ethnic and racial groups. They must be aware of their own privilege, committed to fighting racial injustice, and capable of listening without defensiveness. Allies who fall in this category will be careful not to do harm.

I have intentionally built alliances with women of other races as their perspectives, viewpoints, and experiences sharpen my own. They may also help me understand what

is possible. I want to share a few examples of how relationships with people who are culturally different from me have
impacted my life.

I was newly pregnant when I started my career with a
faith-based organization. I had a ton of anxiety about carrying my second child eighteen years after the birth of my first
child. I was older, and I had switched jobs during my first tri-
mester of pregnancy. I immediately met a woman who served
as an informal coach, helping me navigate the political terrain at my new employer. Dr. Joy Cushman had had a child
when she was around my age, and she was employed with
the company I'd recently joined when she'd gotten pregnant.
When I met Joy, she told me what to expect as an expectant
mom working for a national organization. We discussed how
I would manage long-distance travel, what accommodations I
should request, and which people in the company were most
likely to be supportive. Importantly, she also shared that she
had been allowed to work from home during the end of her
pregnancy and that I should ask for the same thing.

Now the only differences between Joy and me are that
she is white and I am Black, and she is married and I am
not. She and I were both in senior leadership roles: she
was the campaigns director and I was the communications
director. I assumed that if she were permitted to work from
home, I would be too. After all, we both worked hard, and
we were both experiencing high-risk pregnancies. I asked
the chief of staff at my company. She initially said yes,
but then she came back to me, presumably after consult-
ing with human resources, and demanded a doctor's note
before agreeing to my request. I went back to Joy to ask

her if she had been required to provide such a note. She had not. I ultimately obtained the note from my physician, but Joy's willingness to be forthright with me—first about her experiences and then about what appeared to be differing accommodations—helped me understand the racial dynamics at play in the company.

In another situation, a male colleague joked during a conference call that I was using my pregnancy to get "special treatment." For context: I had only been with the company for one month, was experiencing a high-risk pregnancy, and was going through it alone. To be clear, my identity as a single parent was not their problem and I do not want to give the perception that it was their responsibility. But I was shocked that the response to me asking to join via phone was met with "You want special treatment" in a faith-based organization. I needed to ask for accommodations, as travel was difficult and could even be dangerous, and suddenly I felt terribly for having done so. Many pregnant women worry about the appearance of slacking off during their pregnancy, so his comment really hit a nerve. I was so shocked that I tried to change the conversation, but he kept going. I ended up hanging up abruptly as the call was ending. I was completely shocked, embarrassed, and humiliated—both that he made the comment and that no one on the call came to my defense.

I didn't know who to call, so I called Joy. She assured me that the "joke" was inappropriate and told me I should report it to the organization's chief of staff. I told her the chief of staff had been on the phone and hadn't said a word. Joy then took it upon herself to call the chief of staff and ask her why she had allowed the comments to go unchecked. This prompted the chief of staff to take the comments seriously, report them to the president of the organization, and get a formal apology. In this situation, it was nice to have support. I am not sure what would have happened if I had been advocating for myself without the support of others.

In another example, I was considering a position in a gubernatorial administration. My friend and supervisor at the time, Amanda Hoyt, and I had discussed the role for which I was applying and the compensation that I should request. Amanda did a little research and found the position I was applying for had been previously offered to a man and that the organization had offered him $100,000. Still unsure of myself and lacking in confidence, I couldn't bring myself to request $100,000. I was making $75,000 at the time, and while I was smart, capable, and experienced, inwardly I questioned whether I deserved to make "that much money."

When the awkward question of desired salary came up, I told my would-be-employer that my salary request was $85,000—$15,000 less than what Amanda and I had discussed.

After the interview, I wanted to share with Amanda every detail . . . except how I had answered the dreaded salary question. Cutting straight to the chase, Amanda asked, "So what did you tell them you wanted in terms of salary?" I answered sheepishly.

What happened next will shock you—or at least it shocked me. Amanda picked up the phone in her office, called the hiring manager, and told him that I was talented, capable, and worth every dollar they paid me. She told the manager that she knew he had offered the position to a man for $100,000 and that she would hate for there to be a perception of gender bias in them paying me $15,000 less even though I was just as skilled, if not more skilled, than the male counterpart. Furious, the hiring manager promptly ended the call. I was proud that my friend and boss advocated for me, but I was also worried I would lose the opportunity. After checking in with multiple people, however, the manager agreed to increase his offer. He offered me $99,840. Technically, it wasn't as much as he had offered the man, but it was close enough for me.

I cannot overstate the importance of that pay increase for me, my family, and my career. For the first time in my life, I had financial breathing room. Additionally, before you can make $150,000, you often need to hit $100,000. When I eventually left that position, I was able to demand more from future employers because I had made more and had the experience to back it up.

These days I would never allow a friend to advocate for me in the way Amanda did, but I am thankful for that experience. As a white woman, she was able to talk to a white male hiring manager in a way that I am not sure I could have at that time in my life. More importantly, I thought to myself, "If she feels this way about me, what is getting in the way of me advocating for myself more forcefully?" It was an experience I will never forget.

Counsel in Community

In addition to professional matters, Black women especially benefit from the counsel that comes from being in community with other women—Black, Indigenous, Latinx, Asian, white. We experience so much responsibility and pressure that it helps to have a community carry the load. The caveat is the women must be doing their own work and be committed to antiracism.

Glory Edim's anthology *Well-Read Black Girl* includes a conversation with playwright Lynn Nottage. In discussing the transformation that happens when we are in communal spaces such as churches and theaters, Nottage says:

> You can't discount what happens when you have bodies sitting in proximity, and how that energy not only transforms what's onstage, but also transforms the DNA of the people who are in the audience. When you read a book, it's a solitary endeavor. You cry by yourself or you laugh by yourself, but no one else has the same experience in the same moment. But in theater, when someone else laughs and you're sitting next to them, that energy literally is transferred from their body into your body. As an audience member, even though the narrative might not change, your presence in the theater could change the way in which that story is told and received. It's magical.

While Nottage was referring to theater, the value of community shows up in many aspects of our lives. And when I talk about community, I am not just talking about having lots of followers on social media. In an increasingly connected world, we can mistake being influential online with having a tight-knit circle offline. But having an abundance of social media followers doesn't mean one has deep relationships.

A 2018 Cigna study on loneliness found that Generation Z (those born between 1995 and 2015) and millennials (those born between 1981 and 1996) reported feeling lonelier than other groups.

Our lives are busier now more than ever. Even for people who long to help others, time is scarce. People are working longer and harder. I fear free time is now looked down upon, with most people reporting working a minimum of forty hours per week and some as much as fifty to sixty hours per week regularly. Our relationships suffer in the process. If Black women are serious about self-care, we must prioritize our relationships. And in some cases, this could mean placing them higher on our list of priorities.

From whom do you regularly receive counsel? What has been the most helpful thing you've learned from personal or professional mentors, coaches, or advisers?

CHAPTER 23

Close the Feedback Gap

We grow with feedback. To thrive at work as a Black woman, we must take acquiring feedback seriously. But here's the catch: do not wait for your manager to share feedback. Proactively ask for it, time and time again. Without doing so, there is no guarantee you'll receive the input necessary to help you identify and manage your growing edges, improve your skills, or navigate your career. As you go about the process of proactively seeking feedback, it's important to understand the factors that make receiving feedback in real time difficult.

Barriers to Feedback

Black women face three roadblocks to receiving feedback. First, hiring managers and those in leadership positions who are fearful of conflict sometimes withhold feedback.

Next, many managers have their own portfolio of work that is so time-consuming and draining that they lack the time and wherewithal to consistently coach and develop their teams. Rather than mentoring their teams, they are in their own rat race of consistently producing. Finally, race and racism often stall critical feedback. This phenomenon works in two ways. Some managers who are fearful of being labeled racist may withhold feedback to employees of races other than their own. On the other hand, biased managers may be unwilling to invest in developing staff of different races.

This trifecta of feedback roadblocks—conflict avoidance, limited time, and racism—can be disastrous for Black women. Let's walk through each barrier and discuss how to overcome it.

Conflict Avoidance

Hiring managers and company leaders sometimes withhold feedback for the same reason the rest of us do: they're afraid of conflict. In one leadership article, a manager said the most common reason managers cite for not giving feedback is "I don't want to upset my direct report and make things awkward." Some supervisors are simply conflict averse: they do not want to upset the apple cart or navigate interpersonal challenges with their teams. Rather than point out areas for improvement or areas to continue investing in, this personality type may find it easier to keep quiet. They decline to share when employees are making mistakes that may impact their long-term career or their tenure at the company.

Should you find that you are not receiving feedback, proactively ask for it. When you ask for feedback, ask for specific examples of areas that you need to change. In addition to examples, ask the person from whom you are soliciting feedback for specific behaviors that they are asking you to examine or change. Without recommendations for actionable steps you can take, you may not know what to do with the feedback when you receive it. It's also important to note that you must repeatedly ask for input until you receive it. If you are not sure how to approach your manager, consider asking colleagues for recommendations on when and how to engage the specific manager or supervisor.

Limited Time

Many supervisors and managers can become so preoccupied with their own workload that they miss opportunities to coach their team members. Many will not make the time to share tips with a new hire that can help them navigate the current environment as well as future workplaces. This isn't because they don't want to; it's because they lack the bandwidth to do so thoughtfully and consistently.

As an aside, I believe this is one of the oft-spoken impacts of capitalism. Capitalism pushes us to produce, produce, produce. It drives us to continue pushing sales and worshipping at the altar of the almighty dollar. When this happens, we become less people-focused and more profit-focused.

And I have news for you: This isn't just a phenomenon we see playing out in corporate America. Nonprofits also drive their teams exceptionally hard. Whereas corporations fight to improve the bottom line and return as much money to share-holders as possible, nonprofits vie for funding and recognition. In the name of securing funding, they sometimes take on more work than they have the bandwidth to service, or they feel they must work in every lane and respond to every crisis. In the end, the people who make the work possible end up drained, burned out, and sometimes disillusioned. There has got to be a better way.

If you find that your boss is overwhelmed and stretched too thin, consider adding "feedback" as an item for some of your check-ins or regular meetings with your supervisor. Your boss is probably bombarded with meetings and multiple demands on their time. If you use the time that you regularly have with them to ask for feedback, you will condition your boss to expect that you'll be asking for their input—and you'll also make it easier for them to provide it since you won't be adding yet another meeting to their calendar. If this doesn't work, or if you do not have regular check-ins, consider inviting your boss to coffee or drinks and ask them if they have recommendations for you to improve.

Please also know that many people will not tell you everything you need to know in one sitting. This means you must ask for feedback repeatedly—although you should be careful to ask at the rate where you can hear it and implement it.

What do I mean? Asking for feedback weekly or even monthly may be overwhelming. You also may not have the time to act on every recommendation. Further, if you are someone who needs to take time processing feedback, consider that as well. Think about your own personality and then ask in accordance with your individual circumstances and personality in mind.

Racism

Race and cultural differences can also impede feedback. Studies show that managers who are fearful of being labeled racist may shy away from giving honest, constructive feedback to Black people and people of color. In a March 4, 2019, *Harvard Business Review* article, "Women of Color Get Less Support at Work. Here's How Managers Can Change That," authors Zuhairah Washington and Laura Morgan Roberts urged mangers to provide honest feedback as a means of supporting women of color, including Black women. Rather than worrying exclusively about how the feedback will be received based on race, gender, and age, managers should think about the long-term development needs of the employee and keep that front and center as they give feedback. I have personally always felt better when managers and friends have couched feedback in language affirming their support for me, belief in me, and desire to see me succeed.

If you sense that cultural differences are impeding the flow of feedback, proactively ask for it, as in the other scenarios, but ask from multiple people. Rather than limiting your requests to your manager, consider asking trusted colleagues and others at work. This is critical because we will not always get everything we need from the people to whom we report. We must get the feedback on our own and proactively look for tools to aid our advancement.

How to Accept Feedback and Change Your Life

Remember that feedback comes in many forms. You can acquire feedback by being in relationship with others. If you build relationships with people across the organization and outside of your company, you will undoubtedly learn from them in direct and indirect ways. You can also receive feedback in a sit-down conversation. If you're in a profession like mine, where you write and pitch for a living, your feedback could come on your work product. Be open to how feedback may come to you, which could be in a formal or an informal manner.

As you request feedback, you should know what you are seeking. You are seeking items that immediately resonate, meaning you have heard them before or you can see truth in what the person is saying. As you accept feedback, think about what portion of the feedback is true for you and then focus on that alone. This is important because not all feedback is true. In a world in which Black women are scrutinized based on our hair, bodies, tone, and communication style, we must remember that racism, sexism, and homophobia all influence our colleagues' perspectives of us. As such, when we receive feedback, we must consider the lens, worldview, and perspective of the people offering the feedback. This is not to say that people who are different culturally are always wrong. I am simply saying that we must be as discerning as possible.

One way to know if an element of feedback is accurate is to determine whether you have heard it before from different people. If you receive the same feedback from multiple people, there is likely an element of truth in what others are saying.

The main things I want you to take away from this are: you need feedback to improve; there are barriers that will make receiving feedback difficult; and you must make acquiring feedback a priority. If you are not receiving input on your performance, that is not necessarily an indication that all is well. That's a sign that you need to ask more, different, and better questions.

Feedback isn't automatic. As Black women, we must go out and get it. Once we receive it, we must then discern what is and what is not applicable to us.

What has been your experience in asking for and receiving feedback?

CHAPTER 24

Listen in Color

Have you ever experienced talking with someone and before you can get your thoughts out, the person with whom you are speaking interrupts you? Have you been in a conversation with someone and the person cuts you off to paraphrase what they *think* you said—only to have their paraphrase be totally off the mark? Chances are the person with whom you were conversing was not actively listening. Active listening is listening fully to both what a person is saying as well as what is left unsaid. It is paying attention to a person's words as well as their body language and tone of voice. It is the process of listening with interest and reflecting to the speaker what you believe you have heard the individual say.

If Black women are to thrive at work and in our personal relationships, we must make active listening an art form. That means that we are constantly evaluating what a person is communicating and gleaning their values and desires based on that communication.

Without active listening, we may miss cues that an organization culture could be problematic for us. Without active listening, we may miss cues that a friend or colleague is struggling in some way and in need of support. Without active listening, we may not take the necessary steps to ensure the people with whom we are in relationship feel heard and valued. And when people don't feel heard and valued, they may harbor resentment and disappointment.

Few conversations are words spoken just to be spoken. When people communicate, they are giving you a sense of what they value or what is important to them. There is the face-level value of what they are saying, as well as the subliminal messages. The hints may highlight what they like and dislike, what they want and expect, and how they want to be treated. In the workplace, as in other areas of our lives, active listening is critical to building trusting and authentic relationships.

A Muscle That Grows with Use

Active listening is one of those skills that most people lack—meaning when a manager comes across a team member who actively listens, that person automatically stands out. In relationships, people who actively listen can build trusting bonds with others. Mental health expert Arlin Cuncic writes this about active listening:

> It allows you to understand the point of view of another person and respond with empathy. It also allows you to ask questions to make sure you

understand what is being said. Finally, it validates the speaker and makes them want to speak longer. It's not hard to see how this type of listening would benefit relationships. Being an active listener in a relationship means that you recognize that the conversation is more about your partner than about you. This is especially important when a relationship partner is distressed. Your ability to listen actively to a partner going through a difficult time is a valuable skill. In addition, active listening helps relationships in that you will be less likely to jump in with a "quick fix" when the other person really just wants to be heard.

Importantly, active listening is listening without the intent or the impact of judgment. Managers who fail to practice active listening may be unable to build trust with their teams or colleagues. Chances are that if individuals are unable to actively listen to their employees, they are unable to practice active listening with others. Active listening is a muscle that grows with use.

Have you ever worked with someone who excelled at active listening? If so, what did the person do during conversations that you truly appreciated?

CHAPTER 25

Build Your Network

When Ursula Burns was the CEO of Xerox, from 2009 to 2016, there were a host of articles in business publications documenting her career and accomplishments. We looked at Ms. Burns, an African American woman, as an example of what was possible. We aspired to experience her level of success. But the truth is that most of us will never get the chance. While the media touted her accomplishment, many weren't honest about the unlikelihood of other Black women following suit. Presently, there are no African American women running Fortune 500 companies. Have you ever stopped and considered why?

Most people associate with people who look and act like them. Most people have networks full of folks like them racially, religiously, and economically. Not only are their networks lacking in diversity, some want to keep it this way. When these leaders learn of job and career opportunities, they share that information with their homogenous networks. Sure, they want to see others succeed, but they have an image of who "others" entail. For too many white men, their networks and their imaginations are devoid of Black women. Instead, their networks privilege white men first and white women second.

If we talk about networking without speaking to the built-in way networking disadvantages Black people, we are being disingenuous and harmful. In a report published by the *American Sociological Review*, authors David S. Pedulla and Devah Pager note, "On its surface, the use of social networks appears race neutral, but patterns of social and economic segregation imply that their influence will consistently disadvantage members of historically marginalized groups." It is not just that Black people must network, white people and people with power must open their networks to Black people and people of color. And when Black people do advance, they must continually ensure that people who look like them advance as well.

We must remember that African Americans receive fewer job leads through their networks, in general, than white applicants. For instance, Pager and Pedulla found that "Job opportunities are often filled without any formal hiring process . . . and, even when such a process exists, the influence of social connections can still be strong."

When we talk about unemployment among African Americans, it is only fair to cite the structural and informal barriers that make getting a job and climbing the career ladder so difficult. Instead, many economists and politicians talk about unemployment and underemployment in the Black community in a way that pathologizes Black people. In a post-COVID-19 world, COVID-19 will be cited as a reason for lower employment numbers without adequate mention of the role of racism in general, racism in networks, and racism in the labor market.

What Does This Mean for Black Women?

First, we must keep in mind that entire systems exist that disadvantage us. This lets us know that sometimes our lack of upward mobility is less about our ability and efforts and more about the way racism plays out professionally. It is not that we are unqualified, it is that we are not seen.

Next, we must never cease cultivating relationships with other Black women and with non-Black women who value inclusivity and fairness. We must build relationships with women of this variety at work and outside of work. We must build relationships with women who will tell us the truth, women who will comfort and support us, and with men who are committed to doing their own antisexism and antiracism work.

As I reflected on what Black women can do to advance professionally, I reached out to political commentator and former small business owner Tezlyn Figaro for her input. She advised the following:

> I recommend Black women build a circle around ourselves. Our job is to strengthen each other in weaknesses. Black women must also know that it is important to show gratitude to the women in our lives who help us. As a political commentator, when people see me on television, they see me. But it's

important people know that it is not just me sitting in the chair. There are a ton of Black women and Black men who have helped me, supported me, and enabled me to get to where I am today. Since the world doesn't show us any gratitude, we have to show double gratitude toward each other.

While we know this, the point bears repeating because it can be the difference between whether we survive or thrive. Additionally, white allies must do a better job of noticing diversity and inclusion vacuums and creating space at the table for persons who are conspicuously absent. This requires a willingness to share power. It requires a willingness to be decentered.

We know relationships and networks matter. We know the ability to cultivate and maintain relationships with others is a key component of success in a host of professions. Such professions include elected officials, bankers, donors, publicists, agents, and radio and TV hosts. People in these professions work to meet and know as many people in their industries and related industries as possible. Their currency is not merely in what they know but who they know. What is less appreciated is the extent to which white people benefit from formal and informal networks with each other and the degree to which Black people are disadvantaged. And I want to note that I am intentionally and exclusively talking to Black people in this section and in this book. Too many times we will excuse our exclusion of Black people by focusing on our inclusion of non-Black people of color. I will not be confused by the shell game. If Black people are not represented, and non-Black people are represented as tokens, there is no progress.

White allies must focus on being allies in every sense of the word. This includes in employment as well as in any instances of racism. Being an ally is not a one-and-done thing: it's a lifelong way of being. It's a commitment to do one's own antiracism work and to do so without expecting recognition or applause. And Black women must vocally advocate for our inclusion. This means calling people who ordinarily would not reach out to us and initiating a relationship. It means starting our own businesses, and it means prioritizing investing in people who look like us. For Black celebrities and Black people with extreme wealth, it means ensuring that the hiring process centers and privileges fellow Black people.

How Should Introverts Cultivate Relationships at Work?

We know prioritizing relationship building and cultivating a network is important. We cannot be in all discussions or at every function, but expanding our network ensures that we have people in as many rooms as possible who are both committed to antiracism and committed to seeing us succeed.

For our part, Black women should prioritize getting to know the people with whom we work: from the person you perceive as having the most to offer to the person with the least perceived power. Admittedly, this advice may appear easy for an extrovert. But how should an introvert, someone who thrives off solitude, approach relationship-building?

I spoke with licensed marriage and family therapist Narkia Ritchie, who runs a private practice in Fairfax, Virginia. Ritchie shared with me that if meeting new people or attending group functions are stressful, introverts should consider how to get into a relaxed body prior to the meeting or event and how to access their resources. "You can get into a relaxed body even though you aren't feeling calm," says Ritchie:

> Introverts get their energy when they're alone. They aren't shy; it is just harder for them to connect. When introverts are put in situations where they are uncomfortable, their stress response elevates. The way to combat this is to use small pebbles, paper clips, stress balls, or other items that will help the body relax. Introverts can also practice paced breathing or square breathing. I also encourage people to cross their legs if they are prone to shaking them and tap their legs in intervals to help them get into a relaxed body. People who clench their fists when they are nervous can hold a small stress ball or Play-Doh. To help introverts prepare for one-on-one meetings, I encourage them prior to the actual meeting to develop a list of questions they might ask the person with whom they are meeting. Having a list of questions prepared in advance will help with the discomfort of going into a new meeting or a meeting with someone you do not know well.

Ritchie acknowledges that group settings like conferences, receptions, and off-site meetings can be stressful for introverts. She encourages clients to connect with one or two people prior to going to the networking event—colleagues who can offer a supportive presence:

If you are introverted and stay to yourself for two weeks and then go to a work function where you don't know anyone, you will feel even more stress. Try to speak to colleagues before the event and ask one or two of them if you all can share a table or meal together. That way when you go to the group event, you are already matched up with one or two buddies. The bottom line is that it is important to be prepared. If you were going on a road trip, you would check traffic patterns, the weather, and have your vehicle checked out. If you have an idea of what the road trip will entail, you will be more prepared and better able to access resources if you need them. Staying too much to yourself and not knowing anyone will only create more anxiety. It is also important to be okay with the fact that you are an introvert. There is no need to feel you need to be like other employees. But it is important to prepare. If you don't want to go out all the time, tell others you've brought your own lunch or that you have a conference call or need to make a call and then pro-pose another time to connect.

Some of the best leaders in the world are people who have nailed the art of relationship-building. They are genu-inely curious about others. They also understand that their success hinges on other people. You have seen these people. They embrace strangers and friends alike. With ease, they get enveloped in conversations everywhere they go. It's not just that they have nailed the art of communicating with others, they also thrive on it. They are deeply interested in people, and that interest inspires others to want to engage with them.

People who wish to excel in the workplace need this skill. A fancy title does not necessarily confer influence, and people are much more likely to follow a leader they believe respects them than they are to follow someone they believe is uninterested.

As you cultivate relationships, remember that this book is not just another leadership to-do list. Black women can be mindful of the regular tips we are often given to be successful, but we must still navigate sexism, racism, patriarchy, and a host of other challenges. Remember that Black women must scale several mountains in order to make a living, take care of ourselves and our families, and maintain a modicum of happiness in a world based on patriarchy, capitalism, and white supremacy.

I want to challenge you further. Since our needs are different, our antidotes must be unique as well. Consider creating a Black Women's Photo Collage. This is a visual representation of the Black women you meet, hear of, and work with, and who you commit to lifting in prayer. In the same way that some women create a vision board at the start of the year, you can create a photo collage of other Black women who inspire and challenge you and for whom you want to pray. You take pictures of women in your life and post them on foam core or some other poster board. You intentionally leave blank images for the women who will come into your life and for whom you will commit to pray. Then once a week, or at whatever frequency suits you, pray for these women. Pray for their well-being, spiritual growth, and protection from harm. Pray that they have wisdom to navigate their work and home situations, that they find comfort, and, most importantly, that they find a reservoir of support. Once you've created your board, send me a picture of it via social media.

In what ways have you benefited from professional networks? In what ways have your non-Black allies and counterparts benefited from professional networks?

CHAPTER 26

Start Again

Life is filled with ups and downs. We can be flying higher than a kite and then instantly brought low by our own or someone else's actions. There will be good times and not-so-good times. But if we can commit to moving, progressing, and being willing start again, to try again, we will not only make it, we will thrive. If we can remember that life is not a straight line and that our career will not be a direct path either, we will be better than fine.

We will experience challenges that present us opportunities to learn more about ourselves, to refine our approach, and to grow. But if we see the challenges as punishment or if we do not develop the resolve to keep moving forward, we will not experience the richest possibilities of life.

One of my most painful experiences was being transitioned out of a position for an international labor union. I'd moved to Washington, DC, for the role, and the prospect of being in a new city and losing the job that facilitated my move to the area was almost more than I could handle. I kept thinking that losing my job meant that my professional life was ending and there was no hope for a revival.

I recall my last flight for that organization. It was on Frontier Airlines, and I was flying from Wisconsin to Washington, DC. I had rarely traveled before working for the union and saw much of the world on the organization's dime; so in addition to losing my job, I thought I was losing the ticket that allowed me to travel. As I sat on that flight, I tried to savor everything from the sound of the engine turning on, to the sprint down the runway to the clouds high above ground, to the beverage service. I told myself that it would likely be my last flight, so I had better enjoy it. I wish I were kidding. Sure, I knew the Scriptures, and I believed God destined great things for me. But trusting God is a lot easier when things are going well than during upheaval. Reciting Scriptures that urge mustard-seed faith is easy when your bank account is balling out of control. But at that moment, I was a single parent in a new city, and I was losing my job.

I survived, but my survival meant being willing to start again with a new employer. For me, starting again meant looking for and accepting employment that closely aligned with my interests. I was committed to justice, and when a mentor told me about a position at a national racial justice organization, I jumped at the opportunity. I took a $15,000 pay cut for the position and determined that I would work my heart out and gradually earn the salary I had at the union. That is exactly what happened. Within a couple years, I exceeded my prior salary and was not only earning more than I ever had but also was growing professionally. My willingness to accept the lessons from my labor union experience, and to give my all in a new situation, ultimately set me up to succeed.

Admitting that All Is Not Well

Let me offer another example of pushing through obstacles and starting again. I was returning to work after the birth of my second child. I was parenting a newborn alone and managing postpartum depression. I was trying to figure out who I was after having spent so much time focused on my career and now needing to be focused on a helpless infant. When I returned to work after my daughter's birth, I wanted to ease into it. But the workload and the fact that my department was understaffed made doing so impossible. Soon, it wasn't just my home life that was stressful; I was struggling at work as well. I was sleep deprived, depressed, and distracted.

It took me months to admit that all was not well and that I was suffering from postpartum depression and grief for a relationship that I'd desperately wanted to succeed. My work relationships began to fail, there were complaints about my leadership style, and our human resources director at the time wanted to take formal action against me by writing me up. I felt like I was in an impossible situation of needing to perform well at work while sleep deprived and terribly depressed. Things got so rough that I called a friend and told her I wanted to die. While this may sound dramatic, I was proud that I was able to shed the façade of having it all together and be vulnerable.

With suicide being the leading cause of death in the US in 2017, I knew that I couldn't bear my feelings of hopelessness alone. I remember that friend, Amanda Hoyt, somehow talking me off the proverbial ledge. A couple days later another friend, Tomika Anderson, randomly called out of the blue and asked me how I was doing. I was so overwhelmed that I couldn't muster the typical "Fine! How are you?" and decided to be honest with her. She connected me with a counselor, who connected me with another counselor. That counselor was a lifeline and helped me cope with all that I was dealing with. The counselor helped me realize the company I was working for was not a good fit for me professionally and I had to deal with the trauma of being an unsupported single parent. Beginning therapy required vulnerability, patience, and the courage to be honest. This was all in service of understanding that as my life situation changed, my approach to life also had to change. I could no longer throw myself completely into work: I needed to balance caring for a child. I could no longer prioritize everyone other than me: I needed to prioritize myself, which allowed me to prioritize my daughter.

For many people, committing to start again may be the antidote for that bad day, that mistake you feel you can never live down, that career blunder, or that life-altering situation.

I encourage you to keep pushing, even if you can't see how all the pieces of the puzzle align. My message to the rock-star Black women who enjoy outward praise but endure inward pain: have the courage to admit, especially in safe spaces, that all is not well, and take steps to begin again. For the Black women who externally exhibit #blackgirlmagic yet inwardly navigate a web of heartache—or, as political commentator Tezlyn Figaro says, #blackgirlresentment—start again. When it feels as though things can get no worse, perseverance is required.

From one wounded soul to another, the best advice I can give is to start again. Cry it out. Wallow for a time if you must. Then get up and start again.

What has been your experience with starting over?

CHAPTER 27

Remember Who You Are

Throughout this book, I have been honest about the challenges Black women face. I have included the perspectives of several Black women who have shared their experiences that may be like your own experience. We experience racism, sexism, ageism, homophobia, classism, and colorism. In focusing on these areas, my intention is to affirm your experience and suggest that it is not you; it is them. I want to let you know that your experience, while felt individually, represents our collective experience. I have outlined the challenges because I wanted to create sacred space to name what is not discussed enough. But I didn't list the challenges as confirmation that we cannot overcome. We can overcome, and many of us are overcoming. Yet we do so despite numerous obstacles.

To continue to overcome, we need proper perspective. While I have told you what the world is, let me remind you who you are. You are fearfully and wonderfully made. You are the rose that grew from concrete. You are the person in whom others place hope. You are beauty personified. You are glory without effort. You are the one who defied the odds and shattered expectations. You are also the person who made mistakes from which you thought you would never recover. Yet you did. You are a source of inspiration. In your story is many stories. As the first and only, you have created a road map for others to thrive.

In case you have lost confidence in you who are, let me remind you of who God is. Once you get an accurate reading of our Creator, perhaps you can remember that everything that God made, God made well.

In Mark 16:13–16, Jesus stopped by Caesarea Philippi and asked his disciples: Who do people say that I am? The disciples responded, "Some people say that you are John the Baptist and others say you're Elijah. Some people say that you're Jeremiah, and others say you're a prophet." In this moment, Jesus said, "But who do you say that I am?"

I think a lot of Jesus's questions were setups. He would ask a question to draw listeners right into the frame of mind that he wanted them to be. When he is dealing with each of us, he is less concerned about what other people may think and more interested in what we think of him. If we believe, he can work miracles. I share this Scripture to say that even when you have lost sight of who you are and of your abilities, you can draw confidence in who God is. If the spirit inside of you is greater than that which is in the world, know that all you need to be victorious and to thrive will eventually show up. The key is taking things one day, one step, at a time. Try not borrow trouble from the future, but be assured that God can and will meet you in your future and give you provision for that particular time.

I have detailed what it's like to be paid on average sixty-two cents for each dollar a white man earns. But to know something intellectually is not the same as knowing experientially. When you work hard, contribute everything that you can, and yet still earn less than male counterparts, it hurts. When you work in environments where there is little concern and sympathy for what you are experiencing, yet company leaders place loads and loads on your plate, it hurts to know that you are not—and most likely will not—earn what white men and many white women earn. Remember: you are not earning less because you're unqualified. It's because of racism.

I have talked about the risk pregnancy poses to Black women in a world unsympathetic to our needs and conditioned to ignore our voice. This looks like struggling to get doctors, nurses, and health care workers to listen to and act on our needs. It looks like being told to advocate for ourselves without also being told that due to racism, our best argument could be silenced or disregarded.

None of this is easy stuff. Yet I want to remind you that God has given us what we need to thrive. If you personally do not have it, could it be that someone in your circle has it? And when all else fails, if your material needs aren't met, you can always use your voice to powerfully and loudly advocate for what you and your community need.

An Invitation

Finally, I need to remind you that we have been commanded, before now, to be strong. In Joshua 1:9, God tells the people, "Have I not commanded you? Be strong and courageous. Do not be frightened, and do not be dismayed, for the Lord your God is with you wherever you go." If my late aunt Wanda were to say this, she would say, "Didn't God tell you to be strong?"

God invites us to be strong. God said do not be afraid of those who rise against you because the Creator is with you wherever you go.

When you walk into the board room as the first and only, be strong. When you roll into an acquisitions meeting as the unexpected buyer, be strong. When you find yourself a single mother solely responsible for providing the emotional, material, and spiritual needs of children dependent on you for their very survival, be strong. When the people around you are asking you to be strong for them, to take on your share as well as theirs, be strong enough to say, "Not now," or "Not today." Be strong enough to prioritize your needs.

Should you have a mental break and are temporarily unable to keep going, rest in the fact that you do not have to be perfect. You simply must be willing to try again. When they look you up and down and say to themselves, "Who does she think she is?" be strong. When they try to intimidate you into silence and submission, be strong. Find Black women who have modeled the strength that you need in your situation and tell yourself, "If they can do it, so can I."

Now this doesn't mean that you will not break. You will. But as you see yourself slipping, reach out for help. Help can come from a therapist, a sister friend with the capacity and experience to help, or from someone in your spiritual community.

When someone tells you that you are too loud, too aggressive, too assertive, remember that you are never too much. You are just enough. Being strong doesn't merely mean being stoic. It means being resolved. It means being willing to continue trying. It means being able to be vulnerable, especially in safe spaces. You can tell people you are hurting and need help. Not only will this vulnerability help you, it will free others to be vulnerable as well. In fact, vulnerability is a demonstration of your strength, not your weakness. Being strong means being able to say, "I am weak right now."

Being strong means knowing when to quit and when to keep going. You will cry and you will get angry, but be strong. If you believe that you are not strong, remember what has been said about you:

▸ That you were fearfully and wonderfully made.
▸ That God's strength is made perfect in weakness.
▸ That greater is the spirit in you than the spirit that fights against you.
▸ That your Creator will never leave you or abandon you.

Most importantly, being strong is about believing in yourself and believing in God.

What has been the most valuable lesson you've learned as a result of being the first and only?

ACKNOWLEDGMENTS

So many people have supported this work and walked with me as I sought to bring it to the world. Thank you first and foremost to my acquisitions editor, Valerie Weaver-Zercher. Thank you for believing in my work and championing it with your colleagues and friends. Thank you to my editor and strategist, Peppur Chambers. Thank you to my longtime copy editor, Joy Metcalf. Thank you to Malkia Devich-Cyril, Dr. Baranda Fermin, Leslie Pierce, Jarvis Stewart, Theresa Todd, Kim Barbano, Gail Zuagar, and Beulah Osueke, who encouraged my writing and leadership.

Thank you to the Black women who have supported me emotionally and spiritually: Melba Sullivan, Narkia Ritchie, Brittani Strozier, Pastor Trena L. Turner, my sister Sabrina Farmer, and my aunt Gayle Farmer. Thank you to my sister friends Nina Turner, Quanita Roberson, Zakiya Sankara-Jabar, Tori O'Neal, Toni McNeil, and Tezlyn Figaro. You have been wonderful friends and confidantes. Finally, and importantly, thank you to all the Black women who contributed to this book by allowing me to interview them and include their perspectives.

NOTES

CHAPTER 1

For instance, Black women had to work until mid-August 2020: Equal Pay Today website, accessed May 20, 2020, https://tinyurl .com/y8h5pdza. See also Brianne Garrett, "On Black Women's Equal Pay Day, Here's How Women Are Fighting to Close the Gap," *Forbes*, August 22, 2019, https://tinyurl.com/y7ok8ead.

The Southern Poverty Law Center found that Black women: "Weekend Read: Racism Is Killing Black Americans," Southern Poverty Law Center, July 19, 2019, https://archive.is/xptNa.

Dr. Imani Perry, author and professor: Imani Perry, *Breathe: A Letter to My Sons* (Boston: Beacon Press, 2019), 71.

"The truth is that life is unsafe": Perry, *Breathe*, 29.

CHAPTER 2

A November 2019 article in *Variety* reported that Union: Matt Donnelly, "Inside 'America's Got Talent': Ousted Judges Had Complained of Toxic Culture," *Variety*, November 26, 2019, https:// tinyurl.com/vf543hb.

In 1989, when Dr. Kimberlé Crenshaw coined the term *intersectionality*: Kimberlé Crenshaw, "Demarginalizing the Intersection of Race and Sex: A Black Feminist Critique of Antidiscrimination Doctrine, Feminist Theory and Antiracist Politics," *University of Chicago Legal Forum* 1989, no. 1, Article 8, https://tinyurl.com/y6g9znys.

Vox Media reported that Rodriguez: Aja Romano, "Gina Rodriguez Apologizes, amid Backlash, for Saying the N-Word on Instagram," Vox, October 16, 2019, https://tinyurl.com/y3tb8trq .

Column published by NBC Think: Susanne Ramírez de Arellano, "Puerto Ricans' Miss Universe Response Shows Racism Isn't Just for White People," NBC Think, December 15, 2019, https://tinyurl.com/qty3k7x.

The Black Youth Project challenged Ariana Grande in February 2019: Ayika Tshimanga, "How Ariana Grande Uses 'Black Cool' in Her Incremental Appropriation Game," Black Youth Project, February 4, 2019, https://tinyurl.com/y83pzvml.

"The problem of cultural appropriation is": Ijeoma Oluo, *So You Want to Talk about Race* (New York: Seal Press, 2018), 147.

CHAPTER 3

As Audre Lorde said: Audre Lorde, "The Transformation . . .," Genius.com, accessed May 8, 2020, https://tinyurl.com/y7gxtvwd.

Psychologist and professor Angela Neal-Barnett reports: Angela Neal-Barnett, "To Be Female, Anxious, and Black," Anxiety and Depression Association of America, April 23, 2018, https://tinyurl.com/y57h8uu4.

"Women's brains absorb information like pancakes": Heidi Stevens, "Column: Men Are from Waffle House, Women Are from IHOP

— and Other Sexist Nonsense We Learned from Ernst & Young," *Chicago Tribune*, October 23, 2019, https://tinyurl.com/y7vgg7d6.

Researchers Alyssa Croft: Alyssa Croft and Toni Schmader, "The Feedback Withholding Bias: Minority Students Do Not Receive Critical Feedback from Evaluators Concerned about Appearing Racist," *Journal of Experimental Social Psychology* 48, no. 5 (September 2012): 1139–1144, https://doi.org/10.1016/j.jesp.2012.04.010.

CHAPTER 5

There is a reason that Brandt Jean: Domingo Ramirez Jr., "Bothem Jean's Brother Gets Ethical Courage Award for Forgiving, Hugging Amber Guyger," December 3, 2019, https://tinyurl.com/yd8wmvou.

CHAPTER 6

Black women continue to obtain higher education degrees: "Degrees Conferred by Race and Sex," National Center for Education Statistics, accessed May 9, 2020, https://tinyurl.com/y7dvcaqt.

Studies show that Black women: "America's Women and the Wage Gap," National Partnership for Women and Families, accessed May 9, 2020, https://tinyurl.com/ya4m2egs.

CHAPTER 8

former Baltimore mayor Catherine Pugh: "Former Baltimore Mayor Catherine Pugh Facing 11-Count Federal Indictment for Wire Fraud and Tax-Related Charges," United States Department of Justice, November 20, 2019, https://tinyurl.com/sl58no9.

she was sentenced to three years in prison: Brakkton Booker, "Ex-Baltimore Mayor Gets Three Years in Prison for 'Healthy Holly'

Children's Book Scheme," NPR, February 27, 2020, https://tinyurl .com/yd5fva2k.

CHAPTER 12

spiritual teacher and life coach Iyanla Vanzant writes: Iyanla Vanzant, *Trust: Mastering the Four Essential Trusts* (SmileyBooks: Carlsbad, CA: 2015), 8.

The notion that our chronological age could be deceptive: Stephen A. Diamond, "Essential Secrets of Psychotherapy: The Inner Child," *Psychology Today*, June 7, 2008, https://tinyurl.com/yckz2hw6.

CHAPTER 14

Linda Goler Blount, executive director of the Black Women's Health Imperative: Linda Goler Blount, "She Talks Linda Goler Blount," filmed February 2019 at Power Rising Summit 2019, New Orleans, LA, video, 5:05, https://tinyurl.com/y89xwgt2.

Cargle noted that she wanted Black women to rest: Olivia Fleming, "Rachel Cargle Insists Rest Is the Real Revolution for Black Women," *Harper's Bazaar*, November 6, 2019, https://tinyurl.com/yckexgc.

Negative stress not only contributes to ailments: Goler Blount, "She Talks."

CHAPTER 15

Bishop Pearson had a change in theology: Michel Martin, "The Evangelical Christian Who Stopped Believing in Hell, Now on Netflix," NPR, April 15, 2018, https://tinyurl.com/yb26pd25.

Tamar abruptly departed *The Real*: Tamar Braxton, "Sneak Peek: Tamar Gets Real on the New Episode of 'Braxton Family Values,'" *Braxton Family Values*, June 2, 2016, YouTube video, 2:26, https://tinyurl.com/y8esb5p5.

Tracy Brower notes that empathy: Tracy Brower, "Think Empathy Is a Soft Skill? Think Again. Why We Need Empathy for Success," *Forbes*, June 16, 2019, https://tinyurl.com/y7q5zaxu.

CHAPTER 19

Attorney Erika Stallings writes that this phenomenon: Erika Stallings, "When Black Women Go from Office Pet to Office Threat," ZORA, January 16, 2020, https://tinyurl.com/yas8lw8l.

CHAPTER 20

"When we say what is important to us": Soraya Chemaly, "The Power of Women's Anger," filmed November 2018 in Palm Springs, CA, TED video, 11:36, https://tinyurl.com/y9l7bxxh.

Jasmine Tucker, director: Maya Oppenheim, "Black Girls in US Pushed Out of School over Racist and Sexist School Dress Codes, Report Finds," *The Independent*, September 7, 2019, https://tinyurl.com/y832cs83.

Many outlets, including The Guardian: Caroline Davies, "Meghan: I Was Warned British Tabloids Would Destroy My Life," The Guardian, October 21, 2019, https://tinyurl.com/yxst8uw6.

Naturally, when she stopped hosting her show: Jamil Smith, "Melissa Harris-Perry's Email to #nerdland Staff," Medium.com, February 27, 2016, https://tinyurl.com/yah757wz.

"many black churches are willing to pay attention": Monique Moultrie, *Passionate and Pious: Religious Media and Black Women's Sexuality* (Durham, NC: Duke University Press, 2017), 2.

CHAPTER 21

A study on what researchers called "diversity-valuing behaviors": David R. Hekman, Stefanie K. Johnson, Maw-Der Foo, and Wei Yang, "Does Diveristy-Valuing Behavior Result in Diminished Performance Ratings for Nonwhite and Female Leaders?," *Academy of Management Journal* 60, no. 2 (March 2016), https://doi.org/10.5465/amj.2014.0538.

"repeatedly found evidence that our implicit gender perceptions": Maria Konnikova, "Lean Out: The Dangers for Women Who Negotiate," *New Yorker*, June 10, 2014, https://tinyurl.com/ybclztdo.

Bowles and collaborators from Carnegie Mellon: Hannah Riley Bowles, Linda Babcock, and Lei Lai, "Social Incentives for Gender Differences in the Propensity to Initiate Negotiations: Sometimes It Does Hurt to Ask," *Organizational Behavior and Human Decision Processes* 103, no. 1 (May 2007): 84–103, https://tinyurl.com/nkdrwms.

CHAPTER 22

"You can't discount what happens": "'Putting Women Center Stage': A Conversation with Lynn Nottage," in *Well-Read Black Girl*, ed. Glory Edim, reprint ed. (New York: Ballantine Books, 2018), 144.

CHAPTER 23

In one leadership article: Alex Cavoulacos, "3 Excuses Good Managers Use to Avoid Giving Feedback," The Muse, accessed May 12, 2020, https://tinyurl.com/ycvh8lw7.

CHAPTER 24

Mental health expert Arlin Cuncic writes: Arlin Cuncic, "How to Practice Active Listening," VeryWellMind.com, September 27, 2019, https://tinyurl.com/ycuqwu6o.

CHAPTER 25

In a report published by the *American Sociological Review*: David S. Pedulla and Devah Pager, "Race and Networks in the Job Search Process," *American Sociological Review* 84, no. 6 (November 2019): 983–1012, https://tinyurl.com/ydfvbdpk.